Endeavor®

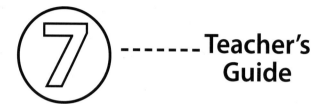

7 ------- Teacher's Guide

New Readers Press®
ProLiteracy's publishing division

2-4

Endeavor 7: Teacher's Guide
ISBN 978-1-56420-875-0

Copyright © 2009 New Readers Press
New Readers Press
ProLiteracy's Publishing Division
104 Marcellus Street, Syracuse, New York 13204
www.newreaderspress.com

Printed in the United States of America
9

Proceeds from the sale of New Readers Press materials support professional
development, training, and technical assistance programs of ProLiteracy
that benefit local literacy programs in the U.S. and around the globe.

Contributing Author: Vista Resources, Inc.
Developmental Editors: Ellen Northcott, Donna Townsend
Creative Director: Andrea Woodbury
Production Specialist: Maryellen Casey

Contents

Strategies for Success with *Endeavor*

Tips for Planning Instruction

There are a number of strategies that you can implement to maximize the effectiveness of *Endeavor's* lesson plans. First, always prepare your lessons before class. This includes reading and practicing the text of the story, selecting activities, and preparing materials. Although the *Endeavor* Teacher's Guide is intended to provide ideas and guidance, it is not meant as a script. Use the explanations in the Teacher's Guide to help you develop explanations in your own words. Additionally, modify the questions, examples, and activities to suit the needs of your students. If, for example, some students need more time to complete an element in the lesson, determine which activities you can omit or shortcut in order for students to have the time they need to be successful. Remember, the objective is for students to feel satisfaction as they become aware of their gains in building reading, writing, and other language skills.

Tips for Implementing Instruction

Students should be clear about what is expected of them. Therefore, inform students of the learning goals and outcomes before beginning a lesson. This Teacher's Guide provides learning objectives on the first page of notes for each lesson. Students should also be clear about how they will perform the tasks required of them. It is imperative, therefore, that you model every new skill, and model skills again if your students have not practiced them in a while. For example, model a sentence that uses a new vocabulary word correctly and in a meaningful context, and then work with students to explain what made your sentence effective. This kind of explicit skill modeling will make your expectations clear to your students. Students will begin to internalize what constitutes a complete answer or a meaningful interaction with a text.

In addition to modeling skills, you will also want to model strategies. Create your own Think About Its to complement those incorporated in the student book. Modeling how you think as you read will provide students with concrete examples of the ways that they should be interacting with text. If you realize that your students have never taken notes as they read, model notetaking. Use a text photocopied onto an overhead transparency and demonstrate how you highlight relevant passages or take notes on the side of the text. The more specific you are and the more examples you give of the various skills and strategies, the clearer the understanding will be in students' minds. Use of the active reading strategies should become second nature to students. This will occur with repetition, so remind them to use strategies that they have already learned.

Fluency and vocabulary development are important components of your students' reading growth. Therefore, you and your students should read aloud whenever possible. Not only will students get to listen to your fluent model and practice their own oral fluency, but students' reading will provide an opportunity for you to do informal assessments. Similarly, the Vocabulary Knowledge Rating Chart (Master 9) can help you to assess your students' facility with words and can inform your vocabulary instruction. If, for instance, most of your students indicate that they fully understand the word *bruised*, but the word *permeated* is unfamiliar, spend your instructional time on the unfamiliar word. Additionally, spend more time on the words that students are likely to encounter in a variety of texts—the key vocabulary words—rather than specialized vocabulary. There are activities and suggestions throughout the Teacher's Guide to assist you in your explanations and planning.

Tips for Maximizing Students as Resources

The life experience of adult learners is invaluable, so make sure that you are bringing students' prior knowledge into every aspect of your teaching. Make your examples relevant to students' experience, and allow them to draw connections between what they are learning and what they already know. The stories and articles in *Endeavor* were selected because they are likely in some way to relate to students' life experiences and concerns. Find those connections, and make them clear to students.

In addition to utilizing students' prior knowledge in your lessons, use students as resources for themselves and one another. The Revising and Editing Checklist (Master 11) is provided as a tool for students. They can check and improve their own and their peers' work using very specific criteria. As always, model the use of the Revising and Editing Checklist, and give students ample opportunity to practice with it. Also, have students use the Writing Rubric (Master 10) to evaluate their completed pieces against measures of ideas, organization, voice, and conventions. Compare your evaluations with theirs as part of writing conferences. These strategies for self- and peer-evaluation do not preclude the need for teacher assessment, but they do give students another set of eyes as they review their own work. The Revising and Editing Checklist and the Writing Rubric allow students to work with and eventually internalize criteria for an acceptable piece of writing.

Assessment is the key to determining if your instruction has been successful and if your students are progressing. You should be using periodic formal assessments, such as the TABE (Tests of Adult Basic Education) or another instrument, to track your students' progress. Informal assessments are important as well, particularly when it comes to modifying your instruction from lesson to lesson. Informal assessments include checklists of skills, over-the-shoulder analyses of students' reading, and your evaluations of students' class work. Although *Endeavor* provides rich resources in terms of texts, activities, strategies, and pedagogy, ultimately it is you, the teacher, who is most important to your students' success. It is your preparation, modeling, and evaluation that will ensure that your students are growing as learners, readers, and writers. We welcome you and wish you luck as you embark on this *Endeavor*.

Suggestions for Developing Vocabulary

Key Vocabulary

The key vocabulary words have been chosen because they are likely to be entirely unfamiliar or somewhat unfamiliar to many students. By working with these words before students begin reading, you are giving students additional keys with which to unlock the meaning of the text. The more they know before reading, the more they are likely to take with them from the reading.

In addition to helping students comprehend a particular text, vocabulary study will provide students with new words to add to their working vocabularies. As their vocabularies grow, they will be able to read increasingly more complex texts. They will also be able to express themselves in a more sophisticated manner in their writing and speaking.

Side-Column Vocabulary

Vocabulary words can be broken down into three tiers. Tier 1 words are the most basic words. These words (like *run*, *need*, and *long*) do not need to be taught, because they are already part of students' vocabularies. Tier 2 words (like *impact*, *inferior*, and *alternative*) are found in more sophisticated texts and across a variety of domains. These are the kinds of words that have been selected as key vocabulary words.

Tier 3 words (like *commute*, *warranty*, and *motorized*) are specialized vocabulary. These words appear infrequently in texts and generally apply only to specific domains. These are the kinds of words that have been selected as side-column vocabulary. Although it will be useful to teach these words in the context of the particular text you are reading, they are not likely to appear frequently or in a variety of texts. Therefore, *Endeavor* focuses more on direct instruction and practice of Tier 2 words than it does on Tier 3 words.

How to Use the Vocabulary Knowledge Rating Chart

The Vocabulary Knowledge Rating Chart (Master 9) is a quick tool for determining students' prior knowledge of each of the vocabulary words. Not only will it help students focus on each of the words, but it will give you a sense of the words on which you will want to concentrate instruction.

Model the use of the Vocabulary Knowledge Rating Chart when you first introduce it. Once students are familiar with the chart, however, they should be able to use it on subsequent sets of words quickly and without extensive instruction.

Tips for Teaching Vocabulary

- The key to learning vocabulary is practice. Each lesson guide includes a number of different strategies for vocabulary practice. Provide as many opportunities as possible for students to interact with and practice the new words.

- Be sure to reframe students' sentences if they are using words incorrectly, and provide additional examples and explanations if necessary. If students learn vocabulary words incorrectly, they will use them incorrectly in the future.

- Use challenging vocabulary when you are talking to your students. Your modeling will help them use words in appropriate contexts, and the unfamiliar words you use will encourage students to explore vocabulary beyond what is being explicitly taught.

- Encourage students to use their new vocabulary words in their everyday lives, and invite them to share anecdotes of when they use the words or encounter the words in conversations or in the media.

Suggestions for Keeping Personal Dictionaries

Personal dictionaries are meant both as spelling aids and as places to record and explore new vocabulary words. For maximum benefit, personal dictionaries should be user-friendly.

A personal dictionary can be created from a notebook or from paper stapled or bound together. It should be its own entity rather than part of another notebook. This will make it more easily accessible and portable as students move through various levels of *Endeavor*. The personal dictionary should be organized alphabetically and have at least four full pages for each letter, perhaps fewer for the less frequently used letters.

Since vocabulary words are best internalized when they are used often, it is important that personal dictionaries be interactive. Students should enter new words they encounter from their experience and from the texts and other print material they are reading. Ask them to include a clear definition and part of speech along with sentences, examples, sketches, or other means for them to internalize

a full, clear meaning of the term. Students should have a voice in deciding what to include in an entry.

Plan frequent activities that require students to return to the words they have recorded. Have students find a "k" word and share it with a neighbor; dramatize a "p" word and have the class guess it; sketch a simple drawing of a word; or write a sentence, correctly using at least three of their vocabulary words. If students simply enter the words and never return to them, the benefit of the personal dictionary will be minimal.

Inside the front and back covers of the personal dictionary, have students record words that are particularly challenging for them to spell. This will limit the number of times they need to search for those words in a large dictionary. It also gives the teacher a place to record words that students are consistently misspelling in their writing. Finally, it ensures that the personal dictionary is being utilized often, as it will be on students' desks as they are writing.

Suggestions for Writing Portfolios

A writing portfolio is intended to hold student work so that the student, teacher, or observer can see how the student has developed as a writer. A portfolio can be a file folder, a box, or a large envelope. Ask each student to create his or her own portfolio. Portfolios can include any writing that the student has done. If the class is producing

a lot of work, you will want to pick and choose items for the portfolio so that it doesn't become unmanageable and unusable. Encourage students to include pieces that they are particularly proud of. The goal is to have the contents organized and accessible.

By reviewing their portfolios, students, and particularly adult students, will have the opportunity to evaluate their own work and growth. They will also have access to the teacher's observations and evaluations of their work. Moreover, portfolios might include copies of the Writing Rubric (Master 10) which students can use to evaluate and comment on their own work. Self-evaluations of final drafts of writing can be modeled by the teacher and done often.

Writing portfolios should be interactive rather than stored out of reach. Students use them to review their work and note their progress. In addition, students should have the opportunity to return to a piece they have written, work to improve it, and then publish it in a creative way. By continuing to interact with their writing and evaluating their own progress, students will remain motivated to improve their writing.

Developing Fluency

Fluency is a reader's ability to recognize words automatically and accurately and to read aloud with appropriate expression. The expression is called *prosody*, and it includes intonation, stress, rate, rhythm, and phrasing. Prosody is important to a reader's understanding of the text. Students must comprehend what they are reading in addition to reading quickly and accurately; therefore, teachers must effectively model and teach prosody. And students need repetition in order to develop fluency.

Although the teacher is an important model of fluent reading, the teacher cannot work individually with every student at the same time. Also, in any group of readers, there are likely to be some differences in students' ability to read orally. Therefore, strategies have been developed to help classrooms of readers at different levels to work on fluency simultaneously. These strategies usually include modeling and repetition.

Fluency in *Endeavor*

Endeavor supports you as you work with your students to improve their fluency. Each lesson in the Teacher's Guide provides strategies you can use to practice fluency. With any of the texts, you may wish to use other strategies in addition to those described in the lesson.

Strategies

Echo Reading—With Echo Reading, students imitate fluent reading modeled by the teacher. The teacher reads aloud, and the students are the echo. Depending upon the level of the readers in your class, you will break the

text into phrases or full sentences. Read the phrase or sentence aloud, paying careful attention to your accuracy and prosody. Then have the class repeat the phrase or sentence, also paying careful attention to accuracy and prosody. Continue reading aloud and having the class echo you for the rest of the passage. Be sure to break the text at logical points in order to maintain the meaning of the text.

Choral Reading—Choral Reading involves students reading aloud together, like a chorus. The teacher begins by reading the chosen passage aloud, concentrating on accuracy and prosody. Then students read the same passage aloud in groups ranging from three students to the whole class reading together. In order to set and maintain the pace, the teacher reads aloud with the students. Choral Reading allows readers the opportunity to practice fluency in a situation where they are supported by other readers.

Paired Repeated Reading—Paired Repeated Reading involves students working with one another—rather than one-on-one with the teacher—in order to improve their fluency. Students work in pairs, and each partner selects a passage to read aloud. Students begin by reading their passages silently. Then partners take turns being the reader or listener. Readers read their passages aloud three times. After the first reading, the listener does not provide feedback. After the second and third readings, the listener provides feedback to the reader.

Be sure to explain and model for students how to give one another constructive feedback. Model directly for students, using a volunteer reader. Tell students that comments such as, "I didn't know from your reading that this sentence was a question" or "I could understand you better if you slowed down and read louder" are more helpful than "Good job." Do a *fishbowl* exercise where the class observes a pair of readers and the class gives feedback on the pairs' feedback to one another. Once students are clear on how to give each other feedback, you will not have to repeat the modeling or fishbowl.

Reading to the Teacher—With small numbers of students in a class, it is possible to give regular attention on fluency to individual students. This gives you a clear sense of each student's strengths and weaknesses. Have students choose passages. Give them an opportunity to review them before they read them aloud to you. Give specific and constructive feedback on accuracy and prosody immediately after the reading. You can also use Echo Reading one-on-one to give students the opportunity for repetition.

Popcorn Reading—With popcorn reading, students take turns reading aloud. Students do not know who is going to be reading next, just as you do not know which kernel of corn will pop next. One student reads a sentence, a few sentences, or a paragraph. Then, he or she says "Popcorn, . . ." and calls another student's name. That student reads part of the passage and then *popcorns* someone else. Students stay on their toes, because they do not know who will be reading next.

Performance Reading—Many students enjoy working in pairs or small groups to dramatize the text they are reading. This strategy works well with texts that include a lot of dialogue. Assign students different roles, and have them practice the dialogue for their characters so that they are able to read their parts fluently and with expression from the text. Then have students perform for the class.

Fluency Tips for the Teacher

- Read and prepare the text before coming to class. It is easier to model fluency if you are already familiar with the text.
- Make sure students are familiar with the text before they begin to work on fluency. If students have already worked with the vocabulary and content of

the text, they will struggle less with pronunciation and phrasing.

- You can use different fluency strategies with the same text. On one day, you might choose to use Echo Reading with a particular story; the next day, you might choose a passage from the same story and do Choral Reading. Remember that repetition is one of the keys to enhancing fluency.

- When pairing students, split the class into two groups according to reading ability. Have the top student of your more able readers work with the top student of your less able readers (conversely, have the low student of your best readers work with the lowest student of your lowest readers.) This may minimize frustration while still providing readers with support.

Keeping Track of Students' Progress

You will want to keep track of your students' reading progress. You can do this by informally recording each individual student's reading accuracy.

- Begin by choosing an unfamiliar passage of about 200 words in length that is at the student's reading level (perhaps from the next lesson in his or her student book or from the student books above or below that level.) Have the student read the passage aloud to you.

- On a separate copy of the same text, put a check mark over each word that is properly read. Each time a reader substitutes, omits, or inserts a word, count it as an error. If the student corrects herself, do not count those words as errors.

- Tally the errors and determine the percentage of words that were accurately read.

- Record a student's reading accuracy every few weeks in order to track progress.

Note: Running Records can be used to do a more thorough analysis of a student's reading and enable you to address individual challenges. You can go online to find explanations and examples of Running Records.

You Can Save Your Own Life

NOTE: Nothing in this lesson should be considered medical advice.

Lesson Overview: (PAGE 5)

Theme

Have students read the lesson title on page 5 and tell them that the title introduces the lesson theme, Health. Discuss the theme by having students make personal connections, telling what they do to stay healthy. Ask students whether they have ever had signs or symptoms that have made them worry or go to the doctor.

Learning objectives

Be sure students understand the outcome of each of the learning goals.

- *Learn about signs that mean you should see a doctor.* The article is relevant to everyone because at one time or another, everyone has to see a doctor. Provide background, explaining that this article is nonfiction. It gives facts based on research.
- *Identify fact and opinion.*
- *Master the key vocabulary used in the article.*
- *Write about what it means to you to take responsibility for your own health.*

Preteach the vocabulary. (PAGE 5)

Read the key vocabulary words and their definitions to the students. Tell them that they will recognize all these words in the article.

- Distribute the Vocabulary Knowledge Rating Chart (Master 9) and have students individually rate each of the key vocabulary words.
- Preview particularly challenging words with students by listing each one on the board, modeling its use in a sentence, and having two or three students use the word in original sentences. Reframe student sentences that do not use the new words correctly.

You may wish to offer a mini-lesson on nouns as students read the respective parts of speech with the definitions of the vocabulary words. [See page 39 of this book for a mini-lesson on nouns. Use Master 1 or 2 to give students practice in recognizing nouns.]

Before You Read (PAGE 6)

Explain to students that good readers get involved with what they read. They learn to select strategies that suit their purpose and that work best for them. They "talk back" to the text and "question the author." This means that they respond to and ask questions about what they are reading. Share with students that the best way to keep track of what they are thinking and of their questions is to keep a pencil or pen in their hands and sticky notes close by.

As students begin to write answers to the questions for each element on page 6, have them read the respective Think About Its.

Ask yourself questions. Have students read the Think About It. Remind students that one way to interact with a text is to ask questions before, during, and after reading. Students should write their questions down and refer to them as answers occur in the text.

Summarize. Have students read the first two paragraphs of "Signs You Can't Ignore" and summarize what they read. Encourage students to stop and summarize what they have read every few paragraphs to ensure that they understand the text. If they cannot concisely summarize the portion of the text, they need to go back and reread.

Reading the Article (PAGES 7–9)

Emphasize to students that they will read to learn the signs of serious illness. This gives them a purpose for reading the article. To keep them involved in the article, suggest that students highlight sentences that discuss indications of a medical emergency. This will help them remember the main ideas so they can apply them to their personal lives.

Side-Column Vocabulary Remind students that the vocabulary words and phrases in the side column have been selected as important to the theme and content of the article. These words may be useful in the context of health and medical problems, but they are not necessarily part of everyday language.

Mid-Passage Questions Some of the answers to the questions call on students' judgments, so there are not many right or wrong answers. Review students' written answers to assess whether they are getting meaning from the text. Students should be able to point to where in the text they have found their answers. They should indicate in their answers that unusually severe headaches should be brought to a doctor's attention, and chest pains that are not spasms are generally not life-threatening.

After You Read (PAGES 10–12)

Build a robust vocabulary. Ask students to check their answers in the answer keys in their books.

Think about your reading. Ask students to check their answers in the answer keys in their books. Ask additional questions to enrich the discussion so that students will be better able to write about solving personal health care problems. Here are some possible questions:

- Sometimes authors use humor in order to connect with their readers. Why do you think the author chose to word this sentence like this: *The food you eat affects the color of your stools, but despite what some people might have told you, black stools are not caused by eating black beans?*

- This article gives basic information about when to see a doctor. Where else can you find information about health-related issues?

Extend the reading. Here are some additional activities to expand students' understanding:

- Have students create a poster or pamphlet that illustrates and explains the symptoms that people should look for when deciding whether they need immediate medical care. Encourage students to include information they have

learned from the article. The goals are to be concise and to educate their readers.

- *For English Language Learners* Have students create flash cards that summarize the various illnesses described in the text. On one side, students will write about and/or draw and label the illness in their first language; on the other, they will write about and/or draw and label the illness in English. This will give students practice summarizing the symptoms, and may also serve as a valuable resource. Have students share their descriptions of the illnesses.

- Point out to students that distinguishing between facts and opinions is very important when deciding whether an illness is urgent and needs medical intervention. Ask students to think of questions that will elicit factual information, such as: *Does the patient have a temperature? Is the patient coughing a lot?* Write the questions on the board. Then have students think of questions that elicit an opinion, such as: *Does the baby look sick? Is the pain in his chest severe?* Ask students to generalize the idea that a diagnosis of illness depends on facts as well as many good judgments.

- At home, have students find articles about strokes, heart attacks, or other health problems. Tell students to read the articles, bring them to class, and prepare to summarize their articles for the next class.

Use reading skills: Identify fact and opinion. Experienced readers of informational text know that authors sometimes write an opinion alongside a fact in order to be more convincing. Readers need to be able to differentiate between facts and opinions so that they are able to make good judgments about what they read. Readers also need to know what the facts are so that they can effectively use the facts to present their opinions in a compelling manner.

Use a graphic organizer. This chart helps readers sort out facts and opinions in the article. In a topic as subjective as personal health, it is particularly important that students be aware of how they arrive at their opinions by first gathering as many facts as possible.

Write About It (PAGES 13–14)

Write your opinion.   Have students read the directions on page 13 and be sure they understand that they will write an opinion paragraph telling what it means to them to take responsibility for their own health.

Prewriting   Remind students that they can organize their paragraphs around the basic topics in the article. These will be the details in their paragraphs. Once students have chosen their details, they can determine the best order for writing the sentences so the details support their opinions. This will help them write their paragraphs in an organized manner.

Thinking Beyond Reading   Have each student work with a partner or a small group to discuss the questions. The intent is for students to probe more deeply and to elaborate on the topic by addressing issues that did not arise when they were first thinking about taking responsibility for their own health. Encourage them to add ideas to their webs.

Write a draft.   Have students write independently. Write on the board the following main idea: *I think I have a responsibility to myself and to my family to stay healthy. Luckily, there are things I can do.* Be sure that students understand that all the sentences in the paragraph must relate to the same main idea, in this case how to take responsibility for their own health. Remind students to use the ideas in their webs to organize their responses. The final sentence should summarize what a person must do

to be responsible. While drafting, students should not be concerned with spelling or punctuation. Encourage them to write their thoughts quickly and freely.

Revise and create a final draft.   Remind students to use the Revising and Editing Checklist (Master 11) to guide them in revising their writing. Have students review each other's writing and give each other feedback on the parts of their paragraphs that are logical, clear, and interesting, and the parts that need revision.

When students have finished revising their writing, use the Writing Rubric (Master 10) to evaluate it. Be sure you review your response with each student so he or she understands the strengths and weaknesses of this piece of writing. Have students date the writing and put the completed pieces in their writing portfolios.

Building Fluency

Identify small sections from "Signs You Can't Ignore." Tell students that they will use paired reading to read these sections aloud. Put students into groups of two. Give them time to read a passage silently 2–3 times to encourage their best oral reading. Partners take turns being the reader or listener. After the first reading, the listener does not provide feedback. After the second and third readings, the listener provides feedback to the reader. Remind students to pay attention to words that cause them to stumble and to read for the author's message. Their goal is to read the passage as fluently as if they were just speaking.

Getting Along at Work

Lesson Overview: (PAGE 15)

Theme

Have students read the lesson title on page 15, and tell them that the title introduces the lesson theme, Work. Discuss the theme by having students make personal connections, telling what kind of work they do or have done and how they feel about it. Have students share situations in which they had to deal with a difficult boss.

Learning Objectives

Be sure students understand the outcome of each of the learning goals.

- *Read a story about a person dealing with a difficult boss.* Point out that the story is fiction, but it deals with the common problem of people getting along at work, especially with the boss.
- *Make judgments about what you read.*
- *Master the key vocabulary used in the story.*
- *Write a paragraph that summarizes the story.*

Preteach the vocabulary. (PAGE 15)

Read the key vocabulary words and their definitions to students. Tell them that they will recognize all these words in the article.

- Distribute the Vocabulary Knowledge Rating Chart (Master 9) and have students individually rate each of the key vocabulary words.
- Preview particularly challenging words with students by listing each one on the board, modeling its use in a sentence, and having two or three students use the word in original sentences. Reframe student sentences that do not use the new words correctly.

You may wish to offer a mini-lesson on adjectives as students read the respective parts of speech with the definitions of the vocabulary words. [See page 41 of this book for a mini-lesson on adjectives. Use Master 5 or 6 to give students practice in recognizing adjectives.]

Before You Read (PAGE 16)

Explain that good readers know when something in a story confuses them, and they take steps to increase understanding. Point out that good readers focus on the reading, putting question marks in the margin where they find things they do not understand. After marking a confusing passage, a good reader forms questions and then rereads to find the answers. Rereading also helps reduce confusion about a character's motivations or other elements in a story's plot.

As students begin to write answers to the questions for each element on page 16, have them read aloud the respective Think About Its.

Use what you know. Use the Think About It to discuss students' experiences with difficult bosses, and how the students dealt with them. What are some different characteristics of bosses who make their employees unhappy? Do different people have different responses to challenging bosses?

Predict what will happen. Ask students how they think Al's boss might be unfair. Do they think that Al is likely to leave his job because of his difficult boss? Point out that they should check whether their predictions are correct as they read the story. Seeing if their predictions are right is one way to be an active reader.

Reading the Story (PAGES 17–19)

Suggest that students read to find how Al reacts to his situation. It is a question to answer as they read. To keep them involved in the story, suggest that they highlight or mark clues that indicate whether Al will leave or stay on the job.

Side-Column Vocabulary Remind students that the vocabulary words and phrases in the side column have been selected as important to the theme and content of the story. These words may be useful in the context of jobs and work, but they are not necessarily part of everyday language.

Mid-Passage Questions The answers to the questions call on students' judgments, so there are no right or wrong answers. Review students' written answers to assess whether they are getting meaning from the text. They should indicate in their answers whether they would have done what Tami did, and whether they expected that Steve and Al would provoke each other again as the tensions built.

After You Read (PAGES 20–22)

Build a robust vocabulary. Ask students to check their answers in the answer keys in their books.

Think about your reading. Ask students to check their answers in the answer keys in their books. Ask additional questions to enrich the discussion so that students will be better able to write about dealing with a difficult boss. Here are some possible questions:

- A good reader reads "between the lines." Sometimes a writer provides hints or makes cultural references rather than saying things directly. What does the author mean by: "Now they were living just on his salary, not exactly Bill Gates wages"? What is another way the author could have written that sentence to have it mean the same thing?

- Al returns home after Steve calls him a moron at work. Al throws a chair across the room and yells. The author writes, "Tami just looked at him sadly." What was Tami thinking? How do you know?

Extend the reading. Here are some additional activities to expand students' understanding.

- Invite students to take parts and dramatize the story. Have students work in small groups to read through the text and highlight important dialogue. Then have them act out the story using the dialogue. Have groups present their dramatizations to the class.

- *For English Language Learners* This story contains a variety of colloquial expressions that do not mean exactly what the words say: *on my back, figure out, gather himself.* Have students find and read the expressions in the context of the story and explain what they think the

phrases mean. Model for them additional sentences that use the phrases correctly until students understand their proper usage in English. Have students try to use these phrases in original sentences. Remind students to add these phrases to their personal dictionaries.

- At home, have each student read or listen to news. Have students summarize a story and then use that summary to form a judgment about the people or situations in the article. Have students share with the class their summaries and judgments.

Use reading skills: Make judgments. Explain to students that experienced readers interact with a text by making judgments about the characters in a story. These judgments are formed as a result of how the reader feels about the characters' actions and words. Students bring their own experiences and values to what they read about the characters. Some students will say that Al should not put up with his boss's unreasonable behavior and he should leave. Others will think that he should learn to accept his boss and value his job in order to support his family. Remind students that there are no right or wrong answers to these questions.

Use a graphic organizer. This chart helps organize events in the story so that students can make clear judgments about the character's actions. Do students agree with Al's decision in both of these situations? The chart is a concrete way for students to interact with the text and to record their individual judgments.

Write About It (PAGES 23–24)

Write a summary. Have students read the directions on page 23 and be sure they understand that they will write a one-paragraph a summary of the story they have just read.

Prewriting Remind students that summaries include just the most important information from an article or a story. A story summary is generally most useful when it is in chronological order. As they review the story, have students use sticky notes to record the most important events. That way, they can add information or switch the order of the events if they need to, although this story is written in chronological order. Students can then place the sticky notes in the graphic organizer in the correct order.

Thinking Beyond Reading   Have students work with a partner or a small group to discuss the questions. The intent is for students to probe more deeply and to elaborate on the topic by discussing the most important events in the story. Encourage them to add ideas to their graphic organizers.

Write a draft.   Have students write independently. Be sure that students understand that all the sentences in the paragraph must relate to the same main idea, in this case how Al dealt with a difficult boss. Remind students to use the ideas in their charts to organize their responses. These will be the details in their paragraphs. While drafting, students should not be concerned with spelling or punctuation. Encourage them to write their thoughts quickly and freely.

Revise and create a final draft.   Remind students to use the Revising and Editing Checklist (Master 11) to guide them in revising their writing. Have students review each other's writing and give each other feedback on the parts

of their paragraphs that are logical, clear, and interesting, and the parts that need revision.

When students have finished revising their writing, use the Writing Rubric (Master 10) to evaluate it. Be sure you review your response with each student so he or she understands the strengths and weaknesses of this piece of writing. Have students date the writing and put the completed pieces in their writing portfolios.

Building Fluency

Identify small sections from "An Awful Boss." Tell students that they will use paired reading to read these sections aloud. Put students into groups of two. Give them time to read a passage silently 2–3 times to encourage their best oral reading. Partners take turns being the reader or listener. After the first reading, the listener does not provide feedback. After the second and third readings, the listener provides feedback to the reader. Remind students to pay attention to words that cause them to stumble and to read for the author's message. Their goal is to read the passage as fluently as if they were just speaking.

The Changing Family

Lesson Overview: (PAGE 25)

Theme

Have students read the lesson title on page 25 and tell them that the title introduces the lesson theme, Family. Discuss the theme by having students make personal connections, telling who they live with now and who lived with them when they were growing up. Ask students if they know families where parents are taking care of both their children and their own parents.

Learning objectives

Be sure students understand the outcome of each of the learning goals.

- *Read an article about the sandwich generation.* Point out that this article is nonfiction. It uses made-up characters to illustrate real situations.
- *Synthesize information.*
- *Master the key vocabulary used in the article.*
- *Write an explanation of how to help aging family members.*

Preteach the vocabulary. (PAGE 25)

Read the key vocabulary words and their definitions to the students. Tell them that they will recognize all these words in the article.

- Distribute the Vocabulary Knowledge Rating Chart (Master 9) and have students individually rate each of the key vocabulary words.
- Preview particularly challenging words with students by listing each one on the board, modeling its use in a sentence, and having two or three students use the word in original sentences. Reframe student sentences that do not use the new words correctly.

You may wish to offer a mini-lesson on nouns as students read the respective parts of speech with the definitions of the vocabulary words. [See page 39 of this book for a mini-lesson on nouns. Use Master 1 or 2 to give students practice in recognizing nouns.]

Before You Read (PAGE 26)

Explain to students that, as they read, they should be deciding which strategies they will use to increase understanding of that particular text. Point out that good readers record their questions or thoughts and highlight phrases that answer a question or address an issue. Suggest that students always keep a pen or pencil, a highlighter, and sticky notes available as they are reading.

As students begin to write answers to the questions for each element on page 26, have them read the respective Think About Its.

Set a purpose for reading. Have students determine what they would like to learn from the article and how that information might be useful to them. If this situation is not yet a reality in students' lives, have them imagine what it would be like to care for children and parents simultaneously. Which generation would take priority? Have students read the first section of the text and then read the Think About It.

Make personal connections to the topic. Students are likely to be familiar with the phenomenon of the sandwich generation, either in their own lives or the lives of the people they know. Ask students to relate to the Think About It by telling how they would deal with a similar situation. Have students practice interacting with the text by inserting a Think About It from their own experience.

Reading the Article (PAGES 27–29)

Emphasize to students that they will read to discover a fuller definition of the "sandwich generation." It is a question to answer as they read. To keep them involved in the article, suggest that students use a highlighter to mark sentences that give useful tips for being responsible at the same time for both aging parents and children.

Side-Column Vocabulary Remind students that the vocabulary words and phrases in the side column have been selected as important to the theme and content of the story. These words may be useful in the context of caring for family members, but they are not necessarily part of everyday language.

Mid-Passage Questions Some of the answers to the questions call on students' judgments, so there are not many right or wrong answers. Review students' written answers to assess whether they are getting meaning from the text. They should indicate in their answers that parents should prepare their children if grandparents are going to be moving in, and that it is important that the parents still have lives of their own.

After You Read (PAGES 30–32)

Build a robust vocabulary. Ask students to check their answers in the answer keys in their books.

Think about your reading. Ask students to check their answers in the answer keys in their books. Ask additional questions to enrich the discussion so that students will be better able to write about caring for different generations of relatives. Here are some possible questions:

- Sometimes, the author expects the reader to fill in the gaps. The author may make a statement, but does not back it up with evidence. What does the author mean by: *Pride may cause them to lie about their ability to take care of themselves?* Explain this statement and give examples of what the author may be talking about.

- The article says that people caring for aging relatives can contact county or state offices for assistance. Where else can sandwich-generation adults turn for help?

Extend the reading. Here are some additional activities to expand students' understanding:

- Have students dramatize a situation in which sandwich-generation adults might find themselves. Have small groups of students write and perform a short skit that illustrates a dilemma that a sandwich-generation adult

might face. Suggest that students be creative in their topics. Guide students to the first paragraph in the text if they are struggling to come up with ideas.

- *For English Language Learners* Tell students that apostrophes tend to be used for two purposes: contractions and possessives. Have students scan the text and make lists of the words that use apostrophes (*She's, aren't, parents', state's, people's, don't, It's, you're*) Have students sort the words into two columns: contractions and possessives. Then have them explain what each word means and use the words in original sentences. Reframe sentences if students use the words incorrectly.

- Remind students that synthesizing means weaving together details that have something in common. Have each student write a short paragraph describing something he or she likes or does not like to do. Each paragraph should include a main idea and at least four details. Then, have students read their paragraphs aloud without including the main idea. The listeners should write or say a topic sentence that synthesizes the information the reader has provided. Then, have the speaker and the listener compare and contrast their topic sentences.

- Outside of class, have each student interview someone who is currently caring for both children and parents. Tell students to identify the person's challenges and rewards. Have students synthesize in a paragraph what they have learned, and then orally share that synthesis with the class.

Use reading skills: Synthesize information. Explain to students that the ability to synthesize is an important skill because it means that you are able to weave information together to formulate an understanding. Many writers begin with a main idea and then generate details to support that idea. When they synthesize, however, some writers, work in the opposite direction: They generate the details and determine what the details have in common in order to write the main idea. Voters who are choosing between two political candidates, for instance, need to synthesize information from the candidates' platforms in order to determine whom they prefer. Otherwise, they are dealing with a lot of little pieces of information that may become confusing.

Use a graphic organizer. In this lesson, the web is a tool that helps students synthesize information about getting ready to have older parents move in. The smaller circles that surround and point to the larger circle are visual representations of what a person can do to prepare for aging parents moving in. The circle in the middle will become the main idea that ties the outer circles together.

Write About It (PAGES 33–34)

Write an explanation. Have students read the directions on page 33 and be sure they understand that they will write in a paragraph an explanation of how to help aging parents. Students will be synthesizing the information in the article into a concise explanation.

Prewriting Remind students that for this assignment, they will choose information from the article that is relevant to helping aging parents. From those pieces of information, they will determine what the main idea is. Have them use the graphic organizer to develop and organize their ideas. It will provide them with a visual representation of those ideas, so it will be easier to determine what the main idea is. Suggest that they keep the central idea as simple as possible.

Thinking Beyond Reading Have students work with a partner or a small group to discuss the questions. The intent is for students to probe more deeply and to elaborate on the topic by making use of other students' ideas and experiences as they consider the different ways to help aging parents. Encourage them to add ideas to their graphic organizers.

Write a draft. Have students write independently. Write on the board the following sample topic sentence:

As parents age, they may need some assistance in order to remain independent. Be sure that students understand that all the sentences in the paragraph must relate to the same main idea, in this case how to aid parents. Remind students to use the ideas in their graphic organizers to organize the different elements of their responses. These will be the details in their paragraphs. While drafting, students should not be concerned with spelling or punctuation. Encourage them to write their thoughts quickly and freely.

Revise and create a final draft. Remind students to use the Editing and Revising Checklist (Master 11) to guide them in revising their writing. Have students review each other's writing and give each other feedback on the parts of their paragraphs that are logical, clear, and interesting, and the parts that need revision.

When students have finished revising their writing, use the Writing Rubric (Master 10) to evaluate it. Be sure you review your response with each student so he or she understands the strengths and weaknesses of this piece of writing. Have students date the writing and put the completed pieces in their writing portfolios.

Building Fluency

Identify small sections from "The Sandwich Generation." Tell students that they will use choral reading to read these sections aloud. (See page 7 of this book for a description of choral reading.) Give them time to read a passage silently 2–3 times to encourage the best oral reading. In order to set and maintain the pace, read along with the students. Identify words that cause the students to stumble. They will imitate the phrasing and intonation that you model. Remind students to use punctuation and typographic cues to add expression to their reading. Tell them that the goal is to read the passage as fluently as if they were just speaking.

Keeping Neighborhoods Safe

Lesson Overview: (PAGE 35)

Theme

Have students read the lesson title on page 35 and tell them that the title introduces the lesson theme, Community. Discuss the theme by having students make personal connections, telling about their communities. Have students share whether or not they feel safe in their communities. Ask them to tell ways in which community members are involved in preventing crime.

Learning Objectives

Be sure students understand the outcome of each of the learning goals.

- *Learn about organizing a neighborhood crime watch program.* Tell students that this article is nonfiction, containing factual information about a well-known, community-based crime prevention program.
- *Draw conclusions about what you read.*
- *Master the key vocabulary used in the article.*
- *Write a letter about a meeting to set up a neighborhood crime watch program.*

Preteach the vocabulary. (PAGE 35)

Read the key vocabulary words and their definitions to students. Tell them that they will recognize all these words in the article.

- Distribute the Vocabulary Knowledge Rating Chart (Master 9) and have students individually rate each of the key vocabulary words.
- Preview particularly challenging words with students by listing each one on the board, modeling its use in a sentence, and having two or three students use the word in original sentences. Reframe student sentences that do not use the new words correctly.

You may wish to offer a mini-lesson on verbs as students read the respective parts of speech with the definitions

of the vocabulary words. [See page 40 of this book for a mini-lesson on verbs. Use Master 3 or 4 to give students practice in recognizing verbs.]

Before You Read (PAGE 36)

Explain that good readers select strategies that help them to stay actively involved as they are reading. Point out that good readers may choose to write down questions and highlight the answers as they read. Or they may choose to summarize. The important thing is that they are not being passive readers. Suggest that students read with a pen or pencil, highlighter, and sticky notes beside them.

As students begin to write answers to the questions for each element on page 36, have them read aloud the respective Think About Its.

Use what you know. Everyone lives in some sort of community, so all the students bring some background knowledge to their reading. Ask, however, what they know about Neighborhood Watch programs. If students are familiar with neighborhood crime watch programs, the title of the article should stir up their prior knowledge. Use the Think About It to elicit discussion.

Set a purpose for reading. Use the Think About It to show that one purpose for reading is to find out how to set up a similar crime watch program that could improve the reader's neighborhood. Once they know why they may be interested in the information in the article, students will be more involved as they are reading.

Reading the Article (PAGES 37–39)

Emphasize to students that they will read to find out how and why people are "taking back their neighborhoods." It is a question to answer as they read. To keep them involved in the article, suggest that students highlight steps that citizens take in setting up Neighborhood Watch programs.

Side-Column Vocabulary Remind students that the vocabulary words and phrases in the side column have been selected as important to the theme and content of the article. These words may be useful in the context of communities and crime, but they are not necessarily part of everyday language.

Mid-Passage Questions Some of the answers to the questions call on students' judgments, so there are not many right or wrong answers. Review students' written answers to assess whether they are getting meaning from the text. They should indicate in their answers that the National Sheriffs' Association runs a nationwide Neighborhood Watch program. Ask students if they think that inviting a law enforcement official to an initial meeting would be an attraction in their neighborhoods.

After You Read (PAGES 40–42)

Build a robust vocabulary. Ask students to check their answers in the answer keys in their books.

Think about your reading. Ask students to check their answers in the answer keys in their books. Ask additional questions to enrich the discussion so that students will be better able to write about setting up a community Neighborhood Watch program. Here are some possible questions:

- The author chose to write as if he or she is speaking directly to the reader. Did this style affect how you read or understood the text?

- Do you think that some communities could benefit more than others from setting up a Neighborhood Watch program? What evidence can you find in the text to support your belief?

Extend the reading. Here are some additional activities to expand students' understanding.

- Have students create posters to advertise a first meeting to discuss a community Neighborhood Watch program. Encourage them to use the information from the article for the text on their posters.

- *For English Language Learners* Have students make lists of plural nouns in the article. Explain the different rules for spellings: regular spellings (the noun + *s,* or *-es*) and irregular spellings (change *y* to *i* and add *es,* or other constructions) Then have students sort the plural nouns into the different types. Discuss the patterns students see. Have students write original sentences, each using a plural noun with a different spelling pattern.

- Guide students in a discussion about associations and organizations that people belong to. Have students describe the purposes or goals of various organizations and what they actually do. Using what students know about each organization, ask them to draw conclusions about the effectiveness of those organizations at achieving their goals.

- At home, have each student determine if there is a Neighborhood Watch program in his or her neighborhood. If there is, ask the student to talk with a few people who are part of the group. With the information provided from those people, the student should draw a conclusion about its effectiveness and share that conclusion with the class. If there is not a Neighborhood Watch program, the student should talk with a few people in the neighborhood and draw a conclusion regarding the possibility of initiating a program. Students can share their conclusions with the class.

Use reading skills: Draw conclusions. Explain to students that effective readers are able to combine information in a text with what they already know to draw conclusions.

Use a graphic organizer. The chart requires the reader to combine what he or she has read with what he or she knows in order to draw a conclusion about Neighborhood Watch groups. The graphic organizer can help students to visually analyze some specific information in the text and the conclusions they can draw.

Write About It (PAGES 43–44)

Write a letter. Have students read the directions on page 43. Be sure they understand that they will write a letter inviting neighbors to a meeting to organize a Neighborhood Watch group. Students will write directly to their neighbors, as if they were just speaking to them.

Prewriting Remind students that neighbors may need to be convinced to come to a meeting, so students are going to need to provide reasons that the Neighborhood Watch is important. Have students fill in the web as fully as they are able, so they will have enough evidence to convince their neighbors to come.

Thinking Beyond Reading Have students work with partners or small groups to discuss the questions. The intent is for students to probe more deeply and to elaborate on the topic by addressing issues that did not arise when they were first thinking about inviting neighbors to a Neighborhood Watch meeting. Encourage them to add ideas to their webs.

Write a draft. Have students write independently. Write on the board the following topic sentence: *Our neighborhood would benefit greatly from a Neighborhood Watch program.* Be sure that students understand that all the sentences in the letter must relate to the same main idea, in this case why the Neighborhood Watch program is important. Remind students to use the ideas in their webs to write their letters. These will be the details. While drafting, students should not be concerned with spelling or punctuation. Encourage them to write their thoughts quickly and freely.

Revise and create a final draft. Remind students to use the Revising and Editing Checklist (Master 11) to guide them in revising their writing. Have students review each other's writing and give each other feedback on the parts of their letters that are logical, clear, and interesting, and the parts that need revision.

When students have finished revising their writing, use the Writing Rubric (Master 10) to evaluate it. Be sure you review your response with each student so he or she understands the strengths and weaknesses of this piece of writing. Have students date the writing and put the completed pieces in their writing portfolios.

Building Fluency

Identify small sections from "Setting Up a Neighborhood Crime Watch." Tell students that they will use paired reading to read these sections aloud. Put students into groups of two. Give them time to read a passage silently 2–3 times to encourage their best oral reading. Partners take turns being the reader or listener. After the first reading, the listener does not provide feedback. After the second and third readings, the listener provides feedback to the reader. Remind students to pay attention to swords that cause them to stumble and to read for the author's message. Their goal is to read the passage as fluently as if they were just speaking.

Everyone Can Read

Lesson Overview: (PAGE 45)

Theme

Have students read the lesson title on page 45 and tell them that the title introduces the lesson theme, School and Education. Discuss the theme by having students make personal connections, telling about their challenges in school including learning to read. Ask students whether they have ever had problems at work because their reading skills were not strong.

Learning objectives

Be sure students understand the outcome of each of the learning goals.

- *Read about a man who struggles to read.* Point out to students that this story is fiction. The characters are not real, but their activities, conversations, and problems are similar to those of people we all know.
- *Compare and contrast.*
- *Master the key vocabulary used in the story.*
- *Write a paragraph to compare and contrast.*

Preteach the vocabulary. (PAGE 45)

Read the key vocabulary words and their definitions to the students. Tell them that they will recognize all these words in the story.

- Distribute the Vocabulary Knowledge Rating Chart (Master 9) and have students individually rate each of the key vocabulary words.
- Preview particularly challenging words with students by listing each one on the board, modeling its use in a sentence, and having two or three students use the word in original sentences. Reframe student sentences that do not use the new words correctly.

You may wish to offer a mini-lesson on adverbs as students read the respective parts of speech with the definitions of the vocabulary words. [See page 42 of this book for a mini-lesson on adverbs. Use Master 7 or 8 to give students practice in recognizing adverbs.]

Before You Read (PAGE 46)

Explain to students that active readers remain involved with the text as they are reading. They respond to the text and "talk" to the author. All active readers ask questions as they read. They write question marks or their questions in the margin when they read things they do not understand. Active reading is best done with a pen or pencil, a highlighter, and sticky notes handy.

As students begin to write answers to the questions for each element on page 46, have them read the respective Think About Its.

Ask yourself questions. Have students read the first paragraph of "To Save a Life" and then read the Think About It. Ask whether students agree that learning how to read can save someone's life, or whether they think the author is exaggerating the importance of the reading class in Cal's life. This is a question they will answer as they read the story.

Reread what you don't understand. Have students reread the first paragraph of the story and highlight the clues that indicate what Cal does for a living. Find out if rereading helped them understand Cal's job better.

Reading the Story (PAGES 47–49)

Emphasize to students that they will read to find out how Cal solves his problem. It is a question to answer as they read. To keep them involved in the story, suggest that students use a highlighter to mark clues to the problems that Cal has and the solutions that he finds.

Side-Column Vocabulary Remind students that the vocabulary words and phrases in the side column have been selected as important to the theme and content of the story. These words may be useful in the context of learning problems and education, but they are not necessarily part of everyday language.

Mid-Passage Questions Some of the answers to the questions call on students' judgments, so there are not many right or wrong answers. Review students' written answers to assess whether they are getting meaning from the text. They should indicate in their answers that Cal is expressing his frustration, and that Mrs. Graves thinks Cal might have dyslexia and wants to see him succeed. Ask students if they think Mrs. Graves can help Cal to become more self-sufficient and confident by improving his reading skills.

After You Read (PAGES 50–52)

Build a robust vocabulary. Ask students to check their answers in the answer keys in their books.

Think about your reading. Ask students to check their answers in the answer keys in their books. Ask additional questions to enrich the discussion so that students will be better able to write about how learning to read better can improve someone's life. Here are some possible questions:

- Authors sometimes want their readers to infer, or figure out things from the characters' actions. What do these actions imply? *Cal threw the thick manual across the room* (page 47), *Cal sighed. He'd heard that before* (page 48), and *Did you get married or something?* (page 49).

- Cal didn't know who to call to get help with his reading problem. Where else do you think he could he have called in addition to the school district?

Extend the reading. Here are some additional activities to expand students' understanding:

- Encourage students to take parts and read some of the dialogues aloud. Encourage students to read with as much natural expression as they can.

- *For English Language Learners* Show students how conjunctions can make speaking and writing flow more smoothly. Have students write the conjunctions *and* and *but* on note cards. Write or say two sentences that can be smoothly joined by a conjunction, and then have students hold up the card that best joins those two sentences. You might say, *I like eggs. I like toast with butter.* Students would hold up their *and* card, and then a volunteer would combine the sentences (*I like eggs and toast with butter.*) using the conjunction. Once students have mastered combining your sentences, have them work in small groups to create and then join sentences using *and* or *but*.

- Point out to students that this story focuses on a young man who changes a lot in the course of the story. Students are aware that they, like Cal, have changed a lot in the last ten years as well. Have students work to compare and contrast themselves today with who they were ten years ago. Have them fill out a Venn Diagram that illustrates how they are the same and how they are different from their younger selves. Remind students to contrast themselves on the same dimensions, such as physical appearance, personality, and jobs. After students have filled out their Venn Diagrams, have them construct compare and contrast sentences that use conjunctions such as *and*, *but*, or *however*, for example, *Ten years ago, I was overweight and had long hair, but today I have lost weight and cut my hair.*

Use reading skills: Compare and contrast. Explain to students that *comparing* is telling how things are similar; *contrasting* is telling how things are different.

Use a graphic organizer. In this lesson, a Venn Diagram offers students a structure within which to compare and contrast the reading they do at home and the reading they do at work. Venn Diagrams can be useful for comparing and contrasting any two things.

Write About It (PAGES 53–54)

Write a paragraph. Have students read the directions on page 53. Be sure they understand that they will write a paragraph that tells how Cal changed and how he stayed the same after he learned how to read.

Prewriting Remind students that learning to read better was a major event in Cal's life. It changed him dramatically, but there were certain elements of Cal that remained the same after he was a better reader. Have students fill in their Venn diagrams as completely as possible, including all of the different dimensions in which the story reported that Cal changed or stayed the same (confidence level, ability to do new work, physical appearance, personality, etc.).

Thinking Beyond Reading Have each student work with a partner or a small group to discuss the questions. The intent is for students to probe more deeply and to elaborate on the topic by addressing issues that did not arise when they were first thinking about how Cal had changed or stayed the same. Encourage them to add ideas to their Venn Diagrams.

Write a draft. Have students write independently. Write on the board the following topic sentence: *Learning to read better changed Cal in some important ways, but in other ways, he was still the same person.* Be sure that students understand that all the sentences in the paragraph must relate to the same main idea, in this case how Cal has changed or remained the same. Remind students to use the ideas in their Venn Diagrams to organize the different elements of their responses. Suggest that they use conjunctions such as *and, also, but,* and *however* to combine their sentences. While drafting, students should not be concerned with spelling or punctuation. Encourage them to write their thoughts quickly and freely.

Revise and create a final draft. Remind students to use the Editing and Revising Checklist (Master 11) to guide them in revising their writing. Have students review each other's writing and give each other feedback on the parts of their paragraphs that are logical, clear, and interesting, and the parts that need revision.

When students have finished revising their writing, use the Writing Rubric (Master 10) to evaluate it. Be sure you review your response with each student so he or she understands the strengths and weaknesses of this piece of writing. Have students date the writing and put the completed pieces in their writing portfolios.

Building Fluency

Identify small sections from "To Save a Life." Tell students that they will use echo reading to read these sections aloud. Put students into groups of two. Give them time to read a passage silently 2–3 times to encourage their best oral reading. Remind them to pay attention to words that cause them to stumble. They will imitate your phrasing and intonation for each sentence. Remind students to use punctuation and typographic cues to add expression to their reading. Tell them that the goal is to read the passage as fluently as if they were just speaking.

A Crime-Fighting Agency

Lesson Overview: (PAGE 55)

Theme

Have students read the lesson title on page 55 and tell them that the title introduces the lesson theme, Civics and Government. Discuss the theme by having students make personal connections, telling what they know about the FBI, the federal law enforcement agency in the United States. Have students share their opinions on whether the FBI is an effective crime-fighting agency.

Learning Objectives

Be sure students understand the outcome of each of the learning goals.

- *Learn about the Federal Bureau of Investigation.* Point out that this article is nonfiction and that it contains factual information about the FBI.
- *Identify main idea and details in what you read.*
- *Master the key vocabulary used in the article.*
- *Write a summary of the article.*

Preteach the vocabulary. (PAGE 55)

Read the key vocabulary words and their definitions to students. Tell them that they will recognize all these words in the article.

- Distribute the Vocabulary Knowledge Rating Chart (Master 9) and have students individually rate each of the key vocabulary words.
- Preview particularly challenging words with students by listing each one on the board, modeling its use in a sentence, and having two or three students use the word in original sentences. Reframe student sentences that do not use the new words correctly.

You may wish to offer a mini-lesson on adjectives as students read the respective parts of speech with the definitions of the vocabulary words. [See page 41 of this book for a mini-lesson on adjectives. Use Master 5 or 6 to give students practice in recognizing adjectives.]

Before You Read (PAGE 56)

Explain that good readers use a variety of strategies. They focus on the reading, putting question marks in the margin where they find things they do not understand. After marking a confusing passage, a good reader forms questions and then rereads to find the answers. Explain that context clues and a dictionary can help with confusing words. Rereading will also help with confusion about an element in the article's content.

As students begin to write answers to the questions for each element on page 56, have them read aloud the respective Think About Its.

Use what you know.   Does anyone have an image of FBI agents as fumbling and humorous? If not, how do students imagine FBI agents? What are the sources of their information? Encourage students to write their own Think About Its in the margin beside the text.

Set a purpose for reading.   Use the Think About It to elicit discussion about how the FBI is portrayed. Do students have respect for the agency? Have students record what they would like to learn from the article on a sticky note. If they have not learned what they wanted to know after reading the article, they can turn to other sources to get more information.

Reading the Article (PAGES 57–59)

Emphasize to students that they will read to learn about the responsibilities of the FBI. To keep them involved in the article, suggest that students underline sentences that describe what the FBI does.

Side-Column Vocabulary   Remind students that the vocabulary words and phrases in the side column have been selected as important to the theme and content of the article. These words may be useful in the context of law enforcement, but they are not necessarily part of everyday language.

Mid-Passage Questions Review students' written answers to assess whether they are getting meaning from the text. They should be able to identify sentences where they have found answers to questions. Their answers should indicate that Americans have sometimes wanted the FBI to have greater powers, and at other times they have been concerned about too much government oversight.

After You Read (PAGES 60–62)

Build a robust vocabulary. Ask students to check their answers in the answer keys in their books.

Think about your reading. Ask students to check their answers in the answer keys in their books. Ask additional questions to enrich the discussion so that students will be better able to write summaries of the FBI article. Here are some possible questions:

- A good reader is able to find the information he or she is looking for within the text. After rereading the last section of the text, describe the typical FBI agent in recent years. How have the requirements changed over time?

- Do you think there is enough glamour in being an FBI agent to help the organization recruit enough people to serve?

Extend the reading. Here are some additional activities to expand students' understanding.

- Guide students to use the information in the article to create a time line of the FBI's history. Students may work alone or in pairs. Have students mark off intervals of 10 years, starting with the 1920s. For each decade, have them concisely summarize the information in the article. Students may wish to do additional research about the decades.

- *For English Language Learners* In order to give ELL students practice in identifying and defining compound words, have them find compound words in magazine and newspaper articles. Remind them that compound words are made up of two words. Ask if their first languages have compound words. Have

students determine what each of the two words means and what the compound word means. Then, have students create original sentences using the compound words.

- Give small groups of students short articles to read. Have students work either individually or in pairs to underline the main idea and put a star next to the supporting details of each article.

- If students know and are comfortable with people who work in law enforcement in their communities (police officers or sheriffs,) ask students to interview them and discuss how the law enforcement professionals see the differences between their jobs and the FBI agents' jobs. Ask students to summarize these conversations for the class.

Use reading skills: Identify main idea and details. Explain to students that identifying the main idea in an article and the details that support that main idea is the key to understanding what one reads. An experienced reader will look for the main idea of each paragraph or each section of an article. As a theme emerges, the reader finds the similarities in the various main ideas and summarizes them, often into one strong sentence. The experienced reader is also able to find the detail sentences that support that main idea.

Use a graphic organizer. In this lesson, the web illustrates how each detail is related to the main idea. The details support the most important idea that the writer wants to communicate.

Write About It (PAGES 63–64)

Write a summary. Have students read the directions on page 63. Be sure they understand that they will write a summary that tells the most important points in the article. Students will need to articulate the main idea of the article and then support the main idea with details from the text.

Prewriting Remind students that most non-fiction text includes a lot of information. There is a main idea for the article, and then the author supports that main idea with details. The point of the summary is to give an overview of the article without getting into too much detail.

Thinking Beyond Reading   Have each student work with a partner or a small group to discuss the questions. The intent is for students to probe more deeply and to consider the main ideas and details they included in their webs. Encourage them to use their webs to sort out the most important ideas to use in their summaries.

Write a draft.   Have students write independently. Be sure that students understand that all the sentences in the paragraph must relate to the same main idea, in this case how the FBI has changed and become more important over the decades. Remind students to use the ideas in their webs to write their summaries. These will be the details in their paragraphs. While drafting, students should not be concerned with spelling or punctuation. Encourage them to write their thoughts quickly and freely.

Revise and create a final draft.   Remind students to use the Revising and Editing Checklist (Master 11) to guide them in revising their writing. Have students review each other's writing and give each other feedback on the parts of their summaries that are logical, clear, and interesting, and the parts that need revision.

When students have finished revising their writing, use the Writing Rubric (Master 10) to evaluate it. Be sure you review your response with each student so he or she understands the strengths and weaknesses of this piece of writing. Have students date the writing and put the completed pieces in their writing portfolios.

Building Fluency

Identify small sections from "Open Up. It's the FBI!" Tell students that they will use paired reading to read these sections aloud. Put students into groups of two. Give them time to read a passage silently 2–3 times to encourage their best oral reading. Partners take turns being the reader or listener. After the first reading, the listener does not provide feedback. After the second and third readings, the listener provides feedback to the reader. Remind students to pay attention to words that cause them to stumble and to read for the author's message. Their goal is to read the passage as fluently as if they were just speaking.

Opportunities Lost and Found

Lesson Overview: (PAGE 65)

Theme

Have students read the lesson title on page 65 and tell them that the title introduces the lesson theme, Sports and Recreation. Discuss the theme by having students make personal connections, telling which sports they enjoy watching and playing. Ask students whether they have ever watched or participated in a particularly exciting or stressful game.

Learning Objectives

Be sure students understand the outcome of each of the learning goals.

- *Read a story about a streetball tournament.* Point out to students that this story is fiction. The characters are not real, but their activities, conversations, and problems are similar to those of real people.
- *Make inferences.*
- *Master the key vocabulary used in the story.*
- *Write a paragraph about sports.*

Preteach the vocabulary. (PAGE 65)

Read the key vocabulary words and their definitions to students. Tell them that they will recognize all these words in the story.

- Distribute the Vocabulary Knowledge Rating Chart (Master 9) and have students individually rate each of the key vocabulary words.
- Preview particularly challenging words with students by listing each one on the board, modeling its use in a sentence, and having two or three students use the word in original sentences. Reframe student sentences that do not use the new words correctly.

You may wish to offer a mini-lesson on adverbs as students read the respective parts of speech with the definitions of the vocabulary words. [See page 42 of this book for a mini-lesson on adverbs. Use Master 7 or 8 to give students practice in recognizing adverbs.]

Before You Read (PAGE 66)

Explain to students that good readers read with a pen, pencil, or highlighter in their hands, and they write as they are reading. They do not passively take in the text. They are constantly summarizing, visualizing, and questioning what they read. Good readers know when they don't understand something, and they take steps to increase their understanding. Suggest that a dictionary can help them figure out challenging words. Rereading will also help with confusion about an element in the story's plot.

As students begin to write answers to the questions for each element on page 66, have them read the respective Think About Its.

Ask yourself questions. Have students read the first two paragraphs of the story and write two questions that come up for them. Then use the Think About It as a model for what a reader might wonder or think about. Ask students to compare their own questions with the question in the Think About It. Remind students that as long as the questions are related to the text, there aren't any bad questions.

Visualize while you're reading. Have students read the first two paragraphs of the story and then describe what the stoop looks like. Then have students read the Think About It. Have students compare their own visualizations with the Think About It. Encourage students to include as much detail as possible in their visualizations. Explain that visualizing the characters and the action in a story will help them follow and remember what is happening.

Reading the Story (PAGES 67–69)

Emphasize to students that they will read to find out why Friz lost his opportunity to play college basketball. It is a question to answer as they read. To keep them involved in the story, suggest that students use a highlighter to mark sentences that tell what has happened to Friz since he left high school.

Side-Column Vocabulary Remind students that the vocabulary words and phrases in the side column have been selected as important to the theme and content of the story. These words may be useful in the context of sports, but they are not necessarily part of everyday language.

Mid-Passage Questions The answers to the questions come either directly or as inferences from the text. Review students' written answers to assess whether they are getting meaning from the text. Students should be able to identify the part of the text from which their answers came. Students should say that Friz's nickname came from his wild hair. Ask students to tell if they considered the Rockets or the Monarchs the better team.

After You Read (PAGES 70–72)

Build a robust vocabulary. Ask students to check their answers in the answer keys in their books.

Think about your reading. Ask students to check their answers in the answer keys in their books. Ask additional questions to enrich the discussion so that students will be better able to write about a championship game. Here are some possible questions:

- A good reader "reads between the lines." What inferences can you make about Friz from the following sentence: *For the first time in months, T.J. saw something in Friz's eyes. It looked like hope.* Why has Friz been hopeless? Does it seem, from the first section of the story, that he has been taking good care of himself?

- Friz worked hard to achieve his goal of getting to the championship where the NBA scouts would be. Do you think that Friz will get recruited to the NBA? Why or why not? If not, what do you think will happen to him? What evidence do you have to support your opinion?

Extend the reading. Here are some additional activities to expand students' understanding:

- Suggest that students dramatize the first section of the story. Have groups of three work together to deliver the dialogue in order to portray the interaction between Friz, T.J., and Dwayne.

- *For English Language Learners* Share with students that English speakers use a number of abbreviations in everyday speech. An abbreviation uses the first letter of each word in a phrase. Examples are *USA* for United States of America and *NASA* for National Aeronautics and Space Administration. Have students find other abbreviations in the first section of "Slam Dunk" (NBA and DUI), and have them use available resources to determine what those abbreviations stand for. Encourage students to include the new abbreviations in their personal dictionaries.

- Ask students to make inferences about the other characters in "Slam Dunk." Do they think that T.J. had a chance to go to college? In what kind of neighborhood do they think the boys live? Do they think that T.J. and the other boys on the teams go to school or do they work? Ask students to explain how they arrived at each of their answers.

- At home have each student find a sports story in a newspaper or magazine. Have students highlight the words or phrases that the author used to make the story particularly interesting or exciting. In the next class, have students share their articles in small groups and compare the words and phrases the various authors used.

Use reading skills: Make inferences. Explain to students that authors of stories often expect the reader to infer from the characters' dialogue and actions what the characters are thinking and feeling. This requires the reader to combine what he or she knows about human nature with what the characters are doing or saying. Point out that being able to make such inferences is important to becoming a good reader.

Use a graphic organizer. A graphic organizer can help students analyze narrative text in order to understand it better. The visual relationship between the ideas in the text and what the reader brings to the text allows the reader to draw the inference. It helps the reader see the way the text works. Do students think that T.J. deliberately missed the shot?

Write About It (PAGES 73–74)

Write a paragraph. Have students read the directions on page 73. Be sure they understand that they will each write a paragraph describing the game between the Monarchs and the Rockets. Students will need to write the events and outcome of the game, but they should also write in a way that is interesting for their audience to read.

Prewriting Some students may not be familiar with sports writing, so it will be important to provide them with a few examples of articles written by sports writers. Have students reread the section of "Slam Dunk" that includes the game. As they are reading, have students write down on sticky notes the important events. Then, have students organize the sticky notes on the flow chart that is provided and add interesting details or descriptive words.

Thinking Beyond Reading Have each student work with a partner or a small group to discuss the important events in the championship game. The intent is for students to probe more deeply and to elaborate on the topic by addressing points that did not come up when they were first thinking about reporting the game. Encourage them to add ideas to their flow charts.

Write a draft. Have students write independently. Write on the board the following topic sentence: *In a tournament to decide which local streetball team will go to the championships, the Rockets beat the Monarchs, 87–85.* Be sure that students understand that all the sentences in the paragraph must relate to the same main idea, in this case the outcome of the game. Remind students to use the ideas in their flow charts to organize the different elements of their responses. These will be the details in their paragraph. While drafting, students should not be concerned with spelling or punctuation. Encourage them to write their thoughts quickly and freely.

Revise and create a final draft. Remind students to use the Editing and Revising Checklist (Master 11) to guide them in revising their writing. Have students review each other's writing and give each other feedback on the parts of their paragraphs that are logical, clear, and interesting, and the parts that need revision.

When students have finished revising their writing, use the Writing Rubric (Master 10) to evaluate it. Be sure you review your response with each student so he or she understands the strengths and weaknesses of this piece of writing. Have students date the writing and put the completed writing in their writing portfolios.

Building Fluency

Identify small sections from "Slam Dunk." Tell students that they will use paired reading to read these sections aloud. Put students into groups of two. Give them time to read a passage silently 2–3 times to encourage their best oral reading. Partners take turns being the reader or listener. After the first reading, the listener does not provide feedback. After the second and third readings, the listener provides feedback to the reader. Remind students to pay attention to words that cause them to stumble and to read for the author's message. Their goal is to read the passage as fluently as if they were just speaking.

Traveling on Two Wheels

Lesson Overview: (PAGE 75)

Theme

Have students read the lesson title on page 75 and tell them that the title introduces the lesson theme, Transportation. Discuss the theme by having students make personal connections, telling how they get to work and/or school. Ask students if they know anyone who chooses transportation based on the impact on the environment.

Learning Objectives

Be sure students understand the outcome of each of the learning goals.

- *Learn about motor scooters.* Tell students this article is nonfiction and that it contains factual information about increasingly popular modes of transportation.
- *Classify information that you read.*
- *Master the key vocabulary used in the article.*
- *Write a how-to paragraph about how to buy a motor scooter.*

Preteach the vocabulary. (PAGE 75)

Read the key vocabulary words and their definitions to students. Tell them that they will recognize all these words in the article.

- Distribute the Vocabulary Knowledge Rating Chart (Master 9) and have students individually rate each of the key vocabulary words.
- Preview particularly challenging words with students by listing each one on the board, modeling its use in a sentence, and having two or three students use the word in original sentences. Reframe student sentences that do not use the new words correctly.

You may wish to offer a mini-lesson on nouns as students read the respective parts of speech with the definitions of the vocabulary words. [See page 39 of this book for a mini-lesson on nouns. Use Master 1 or 2 to give students practice in recognizing nouns.]

Before You Read (PAGE 76)

Point out to students that good readers "talk back" to a text as they read. Students should develop the habit of reading with a pencil and sticky notes or a small notebook available. They will find that it is always helpful to highlight, underline, and write responses or questions as they read. An involved reader goes back to review his or her notes and markings after reading the passage. A good reader also rereads to try to make sense of any parts that were confusing.

As students begin to write answers to the questions for each element on page 76, have them read aloud the respective Think About Its.

Use what you know. Use the Think About It to elicit discussion about students' transportation habits and the efficiency of their transportation. In discussing their transportation habits, students may discuss the benefits and drawbacks of walking, riding a bike, driving a car, or taking public transportation.

Set a purpose for reading. The Think About It suggests that students read to find out the benefits of buying a motor scooter. The introduction to the story suggests that students read to find out why they may want to replace their cars with other forms of transportation. Ask students to describe their own thinking as they set a purpose for reading the article.

Reading the Story (PAGES 77–79)

Suggest that students read to find out why they might want to replace their cars with another form of transportation. It is a question to answer as they read. To keep them involved in the article, suggest that students highlight sentences that describe the benefits of other forms of transportation or the drawbacks of cars.

Side-Column Vocabulary   Remind students that the vocabulary words and phrases in the side column have been selected as important to the theme and content of the article. These words may be useful in the context of vehicles and transportation, but they are not necessarily part of everyday language.

Mid-Passage Questions   The answers to the questions are largely straight from the passage, so students should be able to point to the sentence or sentences in which they found their answers. Review students' written answers to assess whether they are getting meaning from the text. Students should indicate in their answers that the price of gas makes motor scooters appealing; drawbacks of scooter usage may include exposure to bad weather, busy freeways, and limited speeds; and used scooters are often less expensive.

After You Read (PAGES 80–82)

Build a robust vocabulary.   Ask students to check their answers in the answer keys in their books.

Think about your reading.   Ask students to check their answers in the answer keys in their books. Ask additional questions to enrich the discussion so that students will be better able to write about buying a scooter. Here are some possible questions.

- An author does not always explain each sentence in detail. Why do you think the author warns the reader to: *Make sure the scooter you choose comes from a respected company, and that it is covered by a warranty?* What does your life experience tell you about this concern?

- This article focuses on motor scooters as an alternative to cars. What are some other environmentally-friendly alternatives to cars?

Extend the reading.   Here are some additional activities to expand students' understanding.

- Suggest that students create a television infomercial about replacing a car with a motor scooter. They can use almost any section of the text to get their ideas. Once students have written their scripts, encourage them to read

with somewhat exaggerated expression and loud, clear voices.

- *For English Language Learners*   Tell students that when we compare two nouns in English, we often use comparative adjectives. Give some examples: *This book is smaller than that book. This tree is more beautiful than that tree.* Have students find examples of comparative adjectives in the fourth paragraph of the "Scooters, Mopeds, and Motorcycles" section of the text (*faster, heavier, larger*) Have students create their own sentences using those and other comparative adjectives. Remind students that to form the comparative form, most often we add -*er* to an adjective if it has one or two syllables; with three or more syllables, we usually say *more* and then the adjective.

- Guide small groups of students to create charts giving information about their transportation habits. Across the top of the chart have students list their names. In a vertical column, have students enter their own data to answer the following questions: *What is your main form of transportation? How long is your commute? How much do you spend each week on transportation? Is there another way for you to commute?* Have students take turns creating sentences that compare information about the group and the individuals in the group. (*It takes Julio 15 minutes longer than Anita to get to work. Three out of four of us drive a car to work. All of us could choose an alternative form of transportation.*)

- At home, have students write down how much money they spend on transportation and how long it takes them to travel to work or school. Then have them record the same information about at least one alternative travel method. During the next class, have students share interesting facts they discovered about their commutes. Ask whether they believe there is a cheaper, more efficient, or environmentally friendly way for them to commute.

Use reading skills: Classify information.   Experienced readers know that it is easier to remember information if they classify it into categories that are related to each other. The author of "Scooter Story" helped by organizing the information in the first part of the article into useful facts about three different vehicles: motor scooters, mopeds, and motorcycles. How did the author organize the second section? The author wrote the pros and cons of using a motor scooter. How would you classify the main ideas in the last section of the article?

Use a graphic organizer.   Have students work in pairs to complete the graphic organizer. Students will find the information in the text to complete the chart. Partners should ask each other to point to the sentences that give the facts.

Write About It (PAGES 83–84)

Write a how-to paragraph.   Have students read the directions on page 83. Be sure they understand that they will write a paragraph about how to buy a motor scooter. Students will write the steps involved in purchasing a scooter.

Prewriting   Remind students that the information they need is contained in the article; it is their job to find, order, and write the relevant facts from the text. Encourage students to use the chart in order to organize their thoughts. They may wish to use sticky notes so they will be able to reorder the steps if they want to.

Thinking Beyond Reading   Have students work with partners or small groups to discuss the questions. The intent is for students to probe more deeply and to elaborate on the topic by addressing issues that did not arise when they were first thinking about what is involved in purchasing a motor scooter. Encourage them to add ideas to their charts and to revisit the text with their partners.

Write a draft.   Have students write independently. Be sure that students understand that all the sentences in the paragraph must relate to the same main idea, in this case what to do to buy a motor scooter. Remind students to use the ideas in their charts to organize their responses. These will be the details in their paragraphs. Students will need to include transition words to link the details together. While drafting, students should not be concerned with spelling or punctuation. Encourage them to write their thoughts quickly and freely.

Revise and create a final draft.   Remind students to use the Revising and Editing Checklist (Master 11) to guide them in revising their writing. Have students review each other's writing and give each other feedback on the parts of their paragraphs that are logical, clear, and interesting, and the parts that need revision.

When students have finished revising their writing, use the Writing Rubric (Master 10) to evaluate it. Be sure you review your response with each student so he or she understands the strengths and weaknesses of this piece of writing. Have students date the writing and put the completed pieces in their writing portfolios.

Building Fluency

Identify small sections from "Scooter Story." Tell students that they will use paired reading to read these sections aloud. Put students into groups of two. Give them time to read a passage silently 2–3 times to encourage their best oral reading. Partners take turns being the reader or listener. After the first reading, the listener does not provide feedback. After the second and third readings, the listener provides feedback to the reader. Remind students to pay attention to words that cause them to stumble and to read for the author's message. Their goal is to read the passage as fluently as if they were just speaking.

Food Facts

Lesson Overview: (PAGE 85)

Theme

Have students read the lesson title on page 85 and tell them that the title introduces the lesson theme, Food. Discuss the theme by having students make personal connections, telling what kinds of treats they enjoy eating. Have students share what they know about how chocolate is made and where it comes from.

Learning Objectives

Be sure students understand the outcome of each of the learning goals.

- *Learn about chocolate.* The article is of interest to everyone because at one time or another, everyone has eaten chocolate. Provide background, explaining that this article is nonfiction. It presents facts that are based on research.

- *Compare and contrast.*

- *Master the key vocabulary used in the article.*

- *Write an explanation of how chocolate is made.*

Preteach the vocabulary. (PAGE 85)

Read the key vocabulary words and their definitions to the students. Tell them that they will recognize all these words in the article.

- Distribute the Vocabulary Knowledge Rating Chart (Master 9) and have students individually rate each of the key vocabulary words.

- Preview particularly challenging words with students by listing each one on the board, modeling its use in a sentence, and having two or three students use the word in original sentences. Reframe student sentences that do not use the new words correctly.

You may wish to offer a mini-lesson on adjectives as students read the respective parts of speech with the definitions of the vocabulary words. [See page 41 of this book for a mini-lesson on adjectives. Use Master 5 or 6 to give students practice in recognizing adjectives.]

Before You Read (PAGE 86)

Explain that good readers choose strategies to help them get as much from the text as they can. Active readers preview the text, ask and answer questions, and summarize as they read. Since it is difficult to recall all of our thoughts and feelings after we have finished a passage, active readers write as they are reading. They write questions, thoughts, and responses. They also mark meaningful phrases. Active readers get more out of a text than passive readers do, because their minds are constantly working as they read.

As students begin to write answers to the questions for each element on page 86, have them read the respective Think About Its.

Use what you know.   Use the Think About It to elicit discussion about students' feelings about chocolate and where they think chocolate comes from. Do they also know that there are different kinds of chocolate? In answering the questions, many students are likely to convey their fondness for chocolate.

Ask yourself questions.   Have students read the Think About It. Remind students that the Think About Its are models of how active readers respond to text. Since students' prior experiences are different from the models, their questions might be different from this Think About It. What questions would they like to find answers for in the text?

Reading the Article (PAGES 87–89)

Emphasize to students that they will read to learn about the three kinds of cacao beans. It is a question to answer as they read. Putting an asterisk in the margin next to important details is a strategy that will help students stay focused on the information they are seeking.

Side-Column Vocabulary   Remind students that the vocabulary words and phrases in the side column have been selected as important to the theme and content of the article. These words may be useful in the context of chocolate production, but they are not necessarily part of everyday language.

Mid-Passage Questions   The answers to the questions are directly from the text, so students should be able to identify the sentences in which they found their answers. Review students' written answers to assess whether they are getting meaning from the text. Students should indicate that Spanish explorers carried the chocolate drink back to Europe from South America. They may also note that the fermentation process gives chocolate its sweet taste, and that cacao beans are actually quite bitter.

After You Read (PAGES 90–92)

Build a robust vocabulary.   Ask students to check their answers in the answer keys in their books.

Think about your reading.   Ask students to check their answers in the answer keys in their books. Ask additional questions to enrich the discussion so that students will be better able to write about chocolate. Here are some possible questions:

- Reread the preview paragraph for "Chocolate: Food of the Gods." Why do you think the author uses the phrase *dark, delicious history? (wants to get the reader's attention and interest)*

- This article discusses the process for making chocolate and some of the products that come from the ground cacao bean. What are some of the drawbacks of chocolate? *(high-fat food, caffeine)* Why didn't the author address these drawbacks? *(The intention of the article was to talk about why people love the product so much.)*

Extend the reading.   Here are some additional activities to expand students' understanding:

- Ask students to pretend they are guides at a chocolate factory. Have pairs of students find

relevant information from the text about how chocolate is made and include that information in an "informational tour" at a chocolate factory. Remind students to use engaging, clear speech and language as they present their "tours" to the class.

- *For English Language Learners*   Have students look for the different countries mentioned in the article. Have them identify the countries on a map. Lead a discussion about what students know about American history and the explorers who came here from various European countries.

- Point out to students that in this text they had the opportunity to compare and contrast different kinds of eating chocolate and different kinds of cacao beans. Now have students create Venn Diagrams to compare and contrast types of coffee beans. Be sure that students have an opportunity to research coffee beans. Remind students that they should compare and contrast along similar dimensions (e.g. where beans are grown) so that they do not end up with different types of facts about each kind of bean.

Use reading skills: Compare and contrast.   Explain to students that when comparing or contrasting two things or ideas, it is important that they use the same dimensions. For example, the author of "Chocolate: Food of the Gods" noted in the article how easy or difficult it is to grow each of the three types of cacao beans. If a student is noting the color of one item (or its habitat, temperament, etc.), he should also note the color (habitat, temperament, etc.) of the item to which he is comparing the first. This allows readers to make connections and distinctions among the things they are reading about.

Use a graphic organizer.   In this lesson, the Venn Diagram helps students see in what ways cacao beans from Central America are the same as and different from cacao beans from Africa. The graphic organizer highlights the visual relationship between the ideas in the text and helps a reader to see the way the text works.

Write About It (PAGES 93–94)

Write an explanation. Have students read the directions on page 93. Be sure they understand that they will write an explanation of how to produce chocolate candy from cacao beans.

Prewriting Remind students than an important aspect of informational writing is organization. Have students write each step in the process of chocolate-making on a sticky note. Then, have students order the steps within the flow chart. Remind students to go back to the article and make sure that they have included all of the important steps and information. They can also re-order the sticky notes if they want to change the order of the steps they will write.

Thinking Beyond Reading Have each student work with a partner or a small group to discuss the topic. The intent is for students to probe more deeply and to elaborate on the topic by addressing steps or information that they did not originally include when they were writing their sticky notes. Encourage them to add ideas to their flow charts.

Write a draft. Have students write independently. Write on the board the following sample topic sentence: *Making chocolate candy from cacao beans involves many steps.* Be sure that students understand that all the sentences in the paragraph must relate to the same main idea, in this case the process of making eating chocolate. Remind students to use the sentences in their flow charts to organize the different elements of their responses. These

will be the details in their paragraphs. Remind students also to include transition words between the steps. While drafting, students should not be concerned with spelling or punctuation. Encourage them to write their thoughts quickly and freely.

Revise and create a final draft. Remind students to use the Editing and Revising Checklist (Master 11) to guide them in revising their writing. Have students review each other's writing and give each other feedback on the parts of their paragraphs that are logical, clear, and interesting, and the parts that need revision. Have students check each other's work for effective transitions from step to step.

When students have finished revising their writing, use the Writing Rubric (Master 10) to evaluate it. Be sure you review your response with each student so he or she understands the strengths and weaknesses of this piece of writing. Have students date the writing and put the completed pieces in their writing portfolios.

Building Fluency

Identify small sections from "Chocolate: Food of the Gods." Tell students that they will use echo reading to read these sections aloud. Put students into groups of two. Give them time to read a passage silently 2–3 times to encourage their best oral reading. Remind them to pay attention to words that cause them to stumble. Remind students to use punctuation and typographic cues to add expression to their reading. Tell them that the goal is to read the passage as fluently as if they were just speaking.

Being Your Own Boss

Lesson Overview: (PAGE 95)

Theme

Have students read the lesson title on page 95 and tell them that the title introduces the lesson theme, Consumerism and Money. Have students make personal connections by telling if they have ever bought or sold anything at a yard sale. Ask students to share whether they know anyone who has opened his or her own store.

Learning Objectives

Be sure students understand the outcome of each of the learning goals.

- *Read a story about a woman's experience with yard sales.* Point out to students that this story is fiction, but it deals with a popular way of buying and selling things today.
- *Identify cause and effect.*
- *Master the key vocabulary used in the story.*
- *Write a summary of the story.*

Preteach the vocabulary. (PAGE 95)

Read the key vocabulary words and their definitions to students. Tell them that they will recognize all these words in the article.

- Distribute the Vocabulary Knowledge Rating Chart (Master 9) and have students individually rate each of the key vocabulary words.
- Preview particularly challenging words with students by listing each one on the board, modeling its use in a sentence, and having two or three students use the word in original sentences. Reframe student sentences that do not use the new words correctly.

You may wish to offer a mini-lesson on verbs as students read the respective parts of speech with the definitions of the vocabulary words. [See page 40 of this book for a mini-lesson on verbs. Use Master 3 or 4 to give students practice in recognizing verbs.]

Before You Read (PAGE 96)

Explain that good readers constantly interact with the text in a variety of ways. They preview the story, ask and answer questions, and summarize as they read. Since it is difficult to recall all of our thoughts and feelings after we have finished a passage, active readers write as they are reading. Encourage students to develop the habit of reading with a pencil and sticky notes or a small notebook available. These tools help them to keep track of their thoughts and questions, and help them to mark important phrases or sentences.

As students begin to write answers to the questions for each element on page 96, have them read aloud the respective Think About Its.

Ask yourself questions.   Have students read the first four paragraphs of the story and then write a question about the sale Brenda is planning. When students have read the Think About It, ask if they raised the same question: *Will Brenda's yard sale be successful?* Other students will want to know if the sale helped Brenda to successfully clean out her basement.

Summarize what you read.   Have students reread the first four paragraphs of "Glitter and Cash." Then have partners summarize the section in one or two sentences. Have the pairs compare their summaries to see if they express the same ideas.

Reading the Story (PAGES 97–99)

Point out to students that they will read to find out the steps Brenda goes through to prepare for yard sales. It is a question to answer as they read. Highlighting phrases that identify Brenda's planning steps is a strategy that will keep them involved in the story.

Side-Column Vocabulary Remind students that the vocabulary words and phrases in the side column have been selected as important to the theme and content of the story. These words may be useful in the context of buying and selling, but they are not necessarily part of everyday language.

Mid-Passage Questions The answers to the questions are from the text, but they are subject to some interpretation. Review students' written answers to assess whether they are getting meaning from the text. Students should indicate in their answers that Brenda is fed up with the mess in her basement, and she visits other yard sales to buy inexpensive items for resale. They are also likely to mention that she is motivated by Tawna's willingness to give her a commission for all of her hard work.

After You Read (PAGES 100–102)

Build a robust vocabulary. Ask students to check their answers in the answer keys in their books.

Think about your reading. Ask students to check their answers in the answer keys in their books. Ask additional questions to enrich the discussion so that students will be better able to write a summary of the story. Here are some possible questions:

- A good reader "reads between the lines." What did the author want you to figure out from these sentences: *Tawna spread the word. So did Brenda, although she was uncomfortable telling friends they needed to pay her?* Why was Brenda uncomfortable having her friends pay her? How did Brenda get past that discomfort? Would you feel comfortable having your friends pay you a commission for selling their things? Why or why not?

- When there was a drop in sales at Groovy, Brenda got a spot on a local TV show, printed flyers, and got a newspaper writer to write a story about her store. Do you think Brenda did the right things? What were her other options?

Extend the reading. Here are some additional activities to expand students' understanding.

- Have students take turns reading aloud the dialogues in the story. Brenda's and George's conversation in the first section, and Brenda's and Tawny's later conversation offer good opportunities to act out the characters' roles. Some students may prefer to write their own scripts for other sections of the story. Have pairs of students perform for one another. Encourage them to read with as much natural expression as they can.

- *For English Language Learners* Students will benefit from additional practice in identifying and writing common words that end with suffixes. Introduce the suffix *-tion* or *-sion*. Tell students that this suffix generally turns a verb into a noun. Have students find an example of a word with this suffix in the key vocabulary words from "Glitter and Cash" (*satisfaction*). Have students look in other texts, as well, for examples of words with this suffix. Once students have compiled lists, have them write original sentences using their nouns.

- Have students work in pairs to describe something out-of-the-ordinary that happened to them or that they did recently. The listener will chart the causes and effects in the speaker's event and the pair will discuss. Then the pair will switch roles.

- At home, have each student find in a newspaper or magazine an advertisement for a store or business. In class, each student will explain what in the advertisement caught his or her attention. Would they like to go to the store? Why?

Use reading skills: Identify cause and effect. Explain to students that effective readers work to understand a story character's motivations for acting or not acting in particular situations and what impact those characters have on the other characters and the events in the story. For example, would Brenda have organized her first yard sale if George hadn't suggested it? The yard sale was the result (or the *effect*) of George's suggestion. (the *cause*) These events moved the plot forward in the story. Ask students to discuss the relationships between similar events in real life.

Use a graphic organizer.   In this lesson, the cause/effect chart visually organizes important elements in the story's plot, and it helps the reader understand relationships among events.

Write About It (PAGES 103–104)

Write a summary.   Have students read the directions on page 103. Be sure they understand that they will write a one-paragraph summary of "Glitter and Cash."

Prewriting   Remind students that a summary includes the important events and information in the story. Since they will be summarizing a relatively long story into just one paragraph, they will have to make judgments in order to cut out quite a bit of information. Have students think about how they would describe the story events to a friend who asked, "What happened?" Remind them to think in big 'chunks'—the beginning, the middle, and the end of the story. Have students write each of the important plot events on a sticky note, and then use the flow chart to organize the sticky notes.

Thinking Beyond Reading   Have each student work with a partner or a small group to discuss the questions. The intent is for students to sharpen their summaries by adding or deleting ideas that seemed important or unimportant when they were first thinking about how to summarize the story. Encourage them to add or delete events from their charts.

Write a draft.   Have students write independently. Be sure that students understand that all the sentences in the paragraph must relate to the same main idea, in this case all the things that happen when Brenda decides

to clean out her basement. Remind students to use the ideas in their charts to organize their responses. Remind them to determine whether each sentence covers a main idea that should be included in the summary. While drafting, students should not be concerned with spelling or punctuation. Encourage them to write their thoughts quickly and freely.

Revise and create a final draft.   Remind students to use the Revising and Editing Checklist (Master 11) to guide them in revising their writing. Have students review each other's writing and give each other feedback on the parts of their paragraphs that are logical, clear, and interesting, and the parts that need revision.

When students have finished revising their writing, use the Writing Rubric (Master 10) to evaluate it. Be sure you review your response with each student so he or she understands the strengths and weaknesses of this piece of writing. Have students date the writing and put the completed pieces in their writing portfolios.

Building Fluency

Identify small sections from "Glitter and Cash." Tell students that they will use paired reading to read these sections aloud. Put students into groups of two. Give them time to read a passage silently 2–3 times to encourage their best oral reading. Partners take turns being the reader or listener. After the first reading, the listener does not provide feedback. After the second and third readings, the listener provides feedback to the reader. Remind students to pay attention to words that cause them to stumble and to read for the author's message. Their goal is to read the passage as fluently as if they were just speaking.

Grammar Mini-Lessons

LESSON 1: NOUNS

Learning Objectives

To define the term *noun*

To identify nouns

To generate nouns

Activate Prior Knowledge

Help students recall what they know about *nouns*. Ask a volunteer to name the things he or she included on a shopping list during the past week. (Examples: food items, such as *cereal, eggs, meat*; hardware store items, such as *paint, hammer, brackets*) Write the nouns they mention on the board. Ask them the name of the store in which they purchased those items. Remind students that the name of each item and the name of the store are **nouns.**

Instruction

Tell the class that **nouns are the names of people, places, things, and ideas.** Ask students to help you fill out a chart that you have drawn on the board.

Examples of Nouns			
People	Places	Things	Ideas

To begin, ask a volunteer to name a popular athlete. (Examples: *Venus Williams, Muhammad Ali*) Then ask him to decide in which column he would write the name *(people)*. Following the same procedure, ask volunteers to name the places in which the athlete's sport is played *(court, ring)*. Next, ask them to name the equipment the athlete uses in the sport *(rackets, gloves)*. Finally, tell them to name the qualities their popular athlete is known for *(size, speed, skill, tenacity, endurance, grace)*.

If students seem to be having difficulty with nouns as ideas, consider telling them the following: *The names of ideas are not tangible; that is, they are not things that you can touch with your hands. But they are still nouns, just like names of people, places, and things.* Then, to help them generate nouns that are ideas, ask them to try to complete a sentence, such as this: *Venus Williams is known for the _____ she shows on the court.*

Other examples of "idea nouns" might include the names of emotions *(happiness, sadness, excitement, boredom, joy, anger, calmness* or *nervousness)* or character traits *(honesty, sincerity, bravery, timidity, power* or *weakness)*.

When the chart is filled out, ask the class to write sentences, using at least three nouns in each one. Encourage them to try to include a noun that names an idea in each sentence. (Examples: *Venus Williams plays tennis on a court with great speed.* or *Muhammad Ali fought in the ring with amazing skill.*)

Noun Practice

For more student practice with nouns, distribute Master 1 or 2 in this Teacher's Guide.

LESSON 2: VERBS

Learning Objectives
To define the term *verb*

To identify verbs

To generate verbs

Activate Prior Knowledge
Help students recall what they already know about *verbs*. Ask a volunteer to listen closely and then follow your directions. Tell him to stand, walk up the aisle, stop at the front of the class, turn around, smile at the class, and return to his seat. Write the verbs on the board as you say them: *stand, walk, stop, turn, smile, return*. After the volunteer completes the task, point to the board and tell the class that each of those words that indicates an action is a **verb.**

Instruction
Tell students that **words that show action are verbs.** Surprise students by demonstrating that they probably can identify verbs, even if they don't know the meaning of the words themselves. Write on the board this line from Lewis Carroll's poem "Jabberwocky."

> *The Jabberwock, with eyes of flame,*
> *Came whiffling through the tulgey wood*
> *And burbled as it came!*

Invite volunteers to identify the words that show action *(whiffling, burbled)*. Tell them that most people believe they are nonsense words, but they really are verbs that show specific actions. Invite volunteers to guess what action those words might describe. Finally, have a volunteer find them in a dictionary, or tell students what they mean (Merriam-Webster's Collegiate, 11e: *whiffle—to blow unsteadily or in gusts, vacillate; burble—to babble or prattle*).

Write on the board several columns of three words each. In each column include at least one verb. Have volunteers underline the verbs. Warn them that there might be more than one verb in a group. Examples:

<u>swim</u>	shirt	<u>climb</u>	<u>gallop</u>	green	door
comic	<u>scratch</u>	friendly	violin	<u>roar</u>	<u>nap</u>
melon	write	<u>listen</u>	pretty	peace	<u>sweep</u>

Ask students to create oral sentences using the underlined verbs. Challenge them to use as many verbs in one sentence as they can. (Examples: *The cats <u>nap</u> all day long. The children <u>listen</u> to music while they <u>swim</u>. After I <u>sweep</u> the floor, I <u>climb</u> the stairs and <u>roar</u> with laughter.*)

Point out to students that verbs can show time. Write on the board: *All day yesterday I _____ and _____. All day tomorrow I will _____ and _____.* Have them help you fill in the blanks. Then tell them to complete the sentences by adding verbs of their own. Have students say when each of the sentences takes place.

Verb Practice
For more student practice with verbs, distribute Master 3 or 4 in this Teacher's Guide.

LESSON 3: ADJECTIVES

Learning Objectives
To define the term *adjective*
To identify adjectives
To generate adjectives

Activate Prior Knowledge
Help students recall what they already know about *adjectives*. Ask volunteers each to give a two-word description of himself or herself. Start by giving an example of your own: *brown hair*, for instance. Write one or two descriptions on the board. Identify each noun. Underline the word—the **adjective**—that describes it.

Instruction
Tell the class that **adjectives are words that describe nouns.** Elicit from students a list of common nouns. Start by asking whether anyone is a portrait artist or perhaps has seen a police sketch artist on TV. Ask the class to name the features the artist must pay attention to in order to make a lifelike drawing. Make a list on the board.

Adjectives	Nouns
	hair
	skin
	eyes

Have volunteers each write a descriptive word (adjective) in the blank beside the noun. (Examples: *hair—brown, long, curly; eyes—blue, big, clear*) Then invite volunteers to create sentences using a noun and all the adjectives written beside it. (Example: *The man's hair is long, brown, and curly. His eyes are blue and clear.*)

Tell students to write similar lists of their own for a realistic description of a local park. Ask: *What would be listed under "Nouns?"* (Examples: *trees, playground, lake*) *What would be listed under "Adjectives?"* (Examples: *green, sandy, large*) Then have volunteers use their noun-adjective pairs in written sentences. Invite them to share their descriptions with the class.

Adjective Practice
For more student practice with adjectives, distribute Master 5 or 6 in this Teacher's Guide.

LESSON 4: ADVERBS

Learning Objectives
To define the term *adverb*

To identify adverbs

To generate adverbs

Activate Prior Knowledge
Help students recall what they already know about *adverbs*. Ask the class if anyone has ever built dollhouse furniture or a model airplane. Ask volunteers to describe briefly what is involved in building or handling miniatures. Write on the board the verbs and adverbs they use, underlining all the adverbs. (Examples: *first read the directions; work outside; place the parts gently, wait patiently for the glue to dry.*) Tell students that the underlined words are **adverbs.** They describe how, when, and where an action occurred.

Instruction
Tell the class that **adverbs are words that describe verbs.** Draw the following chart on the board.

	ADVERBS		
Verb	**How?**	**When?**	**Where?**

Elicit verbs from the class. Write them in the first column. Then add three adverbs in the other columns. (Example: *build—patiently, today, outside*) For each of their verbs, ask students to provide the adverbs. Encourage them by pointing to and asking the questions at the top of each column. (Example: *Work—How did he work? Quickly; When did he work? Yesterday; Where did he work? Inside;* More examples: *plays—noisily, everyday, there; walks—slowly, always, here*)

Point out to students that adverbs may appear anywhere in a sentence. Often they are close to the verb, but sometimes they are not. Write examples on the board. As you describe where the verb and adverb are located, draw an arrow from the adverb to the verb. Examples:

The clouds <u>aimlessly</u> floated in the blue sky.

The clouds floated <u>aimlessly</u> in the blue sky.

<u>Aimlessly</u>, the clouds floated in the blue sky.

Adverb Practice
For more student practice with adverbs, distribute Master 7 or 8 in this Teacher's Guide.

Master 1: Nouns 1
Student's Name _____

> **A noun is the name of a person, place, thing, or idea.**

Examples of nouns are listed in the chart below.

People	Places	Things	Ideas
sailor	seashore	ship	patience
navigator	universe	compass	bravery

Finding Nouns: Underline the nouns in each sentence. HINT: There are 20 nouns.

1. He delivers newspapers and magazines in the neighborhood.

2. He keeps his earnings in a can his grandmother gave to him.

3. The boy sold his business to an acquaintance for a profit.

4. He knows a quarterback, a shortstop, a forward, and a captain.

5. Though still in school, he works as a waiter on weekends.

6. A young man graduated from college and started a business.

Writing Nouns: Read the nouns below. Write one to complete each sentence.

luck	intelligence	plan	persistence	failure

7. It takes more than _____ to become a success.

8. She must use her _____ to study and learn.

9. It also takes _____ or the will to stick it out.

10. She must not let a _____ keep her from her goal.

11. Her _____ is to do the best she can no matter what.

Using Nouns: Write one noun in each sentence.

12. Experience a trip to the _____.

13. Discover a way to the _____.

14. Reveal the secret of the _____.

15. Draw a map of the _____.

16. Write a letter to the _____.

Master 2: Nouns 2

Student's Name _____

> **A noun is the name of a person, place, thing, or idea.**

Common nouns are the general names for people, places, things, or ideas.
Proper nouns are the names of specific people, places, or things.

	Common Nouns	**Proper Nouns**
People	nurse	Clara Barton
Places	city	Washington, DC
Things	organization	American Red Cross

Finding Nouns: Underline the proper nouns. Remember, a proper noun is often made up of more than one word.

1. William became an aviator for United Airlines.

2. The man is a native of Centralia, a town in Illinois.

3. Norwood was the first African American pilot for that company.

4. His school principal was trained by the Army Air Corps.

5. That man earned his fame as one of the Tuskegee Airmen.

6. The squad members flew over North Africa and Italy.

Writing Nouns: Write the proper nouns in each sentence.

7. Lori was a soldier in the Army Quartermaster Corps. _____

8. She was a member of the Hopi and lived in Arizona. _____

9. She was the first woman killed in the Iraq War. _____

10. Her name in Hopi is White Bear Girl. _____

11. Piestewa Peak, a mountain, is named for her. _____

Using Nouns: Write a proper noun for each common noun.

12. state _____

13. river _____

14. desert _____

15. city _____

16. bridge _____

Master 3: Verbs 1

Student's Name

A verb is a word that shows action.

The underlined words are verbs. They show action.

Subways <u>rumble</u>. Taxis <u>rush</u>. Bikers <u>speed</u>.
Policemen <u>wave</u>. Buses <u>stop</u>. Tourists <u>walk</u>.

Finding Verbs: Circle the verb in each sentence. HINT: Three sentences have more than one verb.

1. He played on the neighborhood baseball team.

2. The player tied the record with seven consecutive hits.

3. One year he amazed the crowds with over 30 home runs.

4. After he batted his best average, he celebrated his success.

5. He walks, hits, and steals bases more than anyone on record.

6. Vote and award him the title of the most valuable player.

Writing Verbs: Write the verb in each sentence. HINT: One sentence has more than one verb.

7. The landmark spans the East River. _____

8. Its stone arches tower above the passageway. _____

9. Construction began around 1870. _____

10. Workers bravely climbed the thick cables. _____

11. Thousands crossed it on the first day. _____

12. It opened in 1883, and still stands today. _____

Using Verbs: For each verb, write another verb with the opposite meaning.

Example: laugh __cry__

13. rise _____

14. lift _____

15. open _____

16. walk _____

17. wash _____

18. yell _____

19. sleep _____

20. stay _____

21. work _____

22. sit _____

Master 4: Verbs 2   Student's Name

A verb is a word that shows action.

The underlined words are verbs.

Verbs	**Time of Action**
A dove <u>perches</u> on a branch.	present
Buds <u>covered</u> each twig.	past
They <u>will bloom</u> in days.	future

Finding Verbs: The verb in each sentence is underlined. Circle the time it shows.

1. The cowboy <u>worked</u> with Will Rogers.   past   future

2. He <u>will perfect</u> the roping technique.   future   past

3. He <u>grabs</u> the steer around the neck or horns.   future   present

4. Then he <u>will throw</u> the bull to the ground.   past   future

5. He <u>wrestled</u> the animal for several minutes.   present   past

6. He <u>earns</u> a place in the Cowboy Hall of Fame.   present   future

7. They <u>created</u> a special stamp to honor him.   past   present

Writing Verbs: Write the verb in each sentence.

8. The men sailed in the wooden boat. _____

9. We will fish for sweet oysters. _____

10. He harvests 40 sacks of them. _____

11. People farmed oysters in Roman times. _____

12. I will enjoy the shellfish next season. _____

Using Verbs: Underline the verbs. Then write each verb to show a different time.

Example: The spider waits for night. ___*will wait*_____

13. The sun pours on the hot dunes. _____

14. A roadrunner dashes over the sand. _____

15. A tarantula scuttles into a hole. _____

16. Ocelots snooze at noon. _____

17. Rain surprises the lizards. _____

18. Toads suddenly appear. _____

Master 5: Adjectives 1

Student's Name

An adjective is a word that describes a noun.

The adjectives in the sentences below are underlined.

Fry <u>two</u> plantains in a pan.
Bite into the <u>tasty</u> chicken.
Serve it with a <u>green</u> salad.

Matching Adjectives: The first column is a list of nouns. Draw a line to connect each one to an adjective. The first one is done for you.

NOUNS   **ADJECTIVES**

1. skyscraper   • heavy

2. people   • several

3. traffic   tallest

4. children   • busy

5. firefighter   • brave

Writing Adjectives: Write the adjective that describes the underlined noun in each sentence.

6. We drove the red <u>truck</u> to the zoo. _____

7. My youngest <u>son</u> watched a tiger yawn. _____

8. A bear tumbled into the icy <u>pond</u>. _____

9. A frisky <u>squirrel</u> jumped over a fence. _____

10. The colorful <u>peacocks</u> pecked at the ground. _____

11. Some <u>monkeys</u> chattered and whooped. _____

12. Our tired <u>feet</u> begged for rest. _____

Using Adjectives: Write an adjective to describe each noun.

13. _____ desk   17. _____ chair

14. _____ walls   18. _____ floors

15. _____ painting   19. _____ lamp

16. _____ rug   20. _____ shelf

Master 6: Adjectives 2

Student's Name _____

> **An adjective is a word that describes a noun.**

The adjectives in the sentences below are underlined.

> <u>Five</u> players are on the <u>open</u> court.
> The <u>best</u> seats are filled with <u>eager</u> fans.
> He wears the <u>blue</u> shirt of their <u>favorite</u> team.

Finding Adjectives: The nouns in each sentence are underlined. Circle the adjectives that describe them.

1. It is the largest <u>city</u> in this great <u>state</u>.

2. The first <u>settlers</u> named it for a major <u>river</u>.

3. Playful <u>comics</u> and serious <u>actors</u> work here.

4. The brilliant <u>colors</u> of autumn surprise us every <u>year</u>.

5. The yellow <u>leaves</u> light up the quiet <u>landscape</u>.

6. Helpful <u>children</u> rake them into tall <u>piles</u>.

Writing Adjectives: Write the two adjectives in each sentence.

7. An old lighthouse sits on a lonely island. _____

8. A sweaty jogger cuts through the empty field. _____

9. The thirsty man bites into a crisp apple. _____

10. The bright flavor of the ripe fruit pleases him. _____

11. Try warm cider with brown sticks of cinnamon. _____

Using Adjectives: Write an adjective to complete each sentence.

12. Climb down the _____ ladder.

13. Jump onto the _____ concrete.

14. Race up the _____ avenue.

15. Stop at the _____ shop.

16. Ask for the _____ pie.

17. Gobble up the _____ dish.

Master 7: Adverbs 1

Student's Name

> **An adverb is a word that describes a verb.**

The underlined words are adverbs. They describe verbs by telling how, when, and where.

He hungrily watches her cook. (watches how?)

She stirs the collard greens often. (stirs when?)

The rich aroma drifts outside. (drifts where?)

Finding Adverbs: Verbs are underlined in each sentence. Circle the adverbs that describe them.

1. Bats live everywhere in the world.

2. Surprisingly, some bats survive in the cold of Alaska.

3. Bats nest here in both city and country environments.

4. They sleep soundly during the daylight hours.

5. A baby bat usually flies at six to eight weeks old.

6. Bats eat mosquitoes, moths, and grasshoppers often.

7. Today many people build bat houses for their yards.

Writing Adverbs: Write the adverbs you circled in the correct column.

How?	When?	Where?
8.	10.	13.
9.	11.	14.
	12.	

Using Adverbs: Complete each sentence with an adverb from the box.

eerily	slowly	bravely	soon	carefully

15. She climbs the steep path _____.

16. Her footsteps echo _____ in the cave.

17. Water _____ seeps into the rocky ground.

18. She _____ explores the dark cavern.

19. She will return _____ to the sunlit surface.

Master 8: Adverbs 2

Student's Name _____

An adverb is a word that describes a verb.

These words are adverbs. They tell how, when, and where.

How?   softly, boldly, gracefully, happily
When? sometimes, tomorrow, never, often
Where? inside, there, everywhere, nearby

Finding Adverbs: The verbs are underlined. Circle each adverb that describes a verb.

1. Carl quickly <u>sprints</u> to the end of the track.

2. He <u>wins</u> both the long jump and the relay race easily.

3. Lewis frequently <u>tops</u> the world rankings.

4. The family gladly <u>moves</u> to a new home.

5. Today he <u>recalls</u> his childhood as a pleasant experience.

6. He greatly <u>admires</u> Jesse Owens, another excellent athlete.

Writing Adverbs: Write the adverb from each sentence.

7. She came here from Jamaica. _____

8. The child wrote in her journal daily. _____

9. The young woman expresses herself well. _____

10. She honestly describes the details of her life. _____

11. I always will remember Anne Frank's diary. _____

12. Both girls touch the reader's emotions deeply. _____

Using Adverbs: Complete each sentence with an adverb from the box.

often	soon	nearby	later	outside	today	again	now

13. Call me _____.

14. Deal with it _____.

15. Let's go _____.

16. Visit her _____.

17. Say it _____.

18. Wake up _____.

19. See you _____.

20. I'll be _____.

Master 9: Vocabulary Knowledge Rating Chart   Student's Name _____

	1	2	3	4	5
Vocabulary Word	I know this word. I can explain its meaning and use it when I speak and write.	I think I know this word. It has something to do with _____.	I've seen or heard this word, but I'm not sure what it means.	I don't know this word. I need to learn it.

Master 10: Writing Rubric

Student's Name _____

	Focus	Organization	Voice	Conventions
4	Ideas are on the topic and interesting.	There is a clearly presented main idea with supporting details, facts, and/or opinions. The writing flows very well.	The writer speaks to the audience clearly. Word choice is varied, and the words were chosen because they are the very best words for getting the point across.	Contains few, if any, errors in grammar, punctuation, capitalization, and/or spelling. Any errors that do occur do not get in the way of the reader's understanding.
3	Ideas are on the topic.	There is a main idea with supporting details, facts, and/or opinions. The writing flows.	The writer speaks to the audience. Word choice is varied and gets the point across.	Contains some errors in grammar, punctuation, capitalization, and/or spelling. These errors do not get in the way of the reader's understanding.
2	Ideas may be a bit off of the topic.	Although there is a main idea and/or details, the writing is sometimes difficult to follow.	The writer shows some understanding of the audience. Words are repeated too often and/or misused.	Contains several errors in grammar, punctuation, capitalization, and/or spelling. These errors may get in the way of the reader's understanding of the writing.
1	Ideas are not on the topic.	It is difficult for the reader to follow the writer's arguments or explanations.	The writer does not speak to the audience. Words are repeated too often and/or misused.	Contains serious errors in grammar, punctuation, capitalization, and/or spelling. These errors make the writing very difficult for the reader to understand.

Master 11: Revising and Editing Checklist   Student's Name

When you **revise,** you add to or take away from your writing to make it clearer and more understandable. It always helps to read your work to a partner so that you can make sure it is well organized, includes enough details, and makes sense.

When you **edit,** look at the specific words you have chosen. Are they the best words? Check your work for proper spelling, punctuation, and usage. Make sure that you have not left out or repeated a word. Have you used correct grammar?

Always revise before you edit. You don't want to spend time editing something you may not include in your revision.

Revising

_____ I read the writing to myself to see if it made sense.

_____ I read the writing to a partner to see if it made sense.

_____ My writing stays on the topic.

_____ My paragraph has a topic sentence and includes supporting details.

_____ My writing is logical and well organized.

_____ The writing is interesting.

_____ I used enough information and examples to make my point.

_____ My ending ties up the writing.

Editing

_____ Each of my sentences ends with a period (.), a question mark (?), or an exclamation point (!).

_____ My subjects and verbs agree.

_____ I have used commas correctly.

_____ Each of my sentences begins with a capital letter.

_____ I have used quotation marks correctly.

_____ My paragraph is indented.

_____ I chose my words carefully so that the reader can visualize just what I'm talking about.

_____ I inserted words that add interest to my writing.

_____ I inserted words that were missing.

_____ I deleted extra words that I didn't need.

_____ I circled words that I think may be incorrectly spelled. I used additional resources to check the spelling of those words.

_____ I gave my edited draft to a partner to check.

Master 12: Editor's Marks   Student's Name

Use these marks when editing a paper. Make sure you understand what the marks mean when a teacher or partner uses them on your paper.

Editing Marks		
≡	Changes a lowercase letter to an uppercase letter.	I visited kiwanis park with my cousins.
/	Changes an uppercase letter to a lowercase letter.	Maria brought her Dog.
∧	Adds a word or punctuation mark.	We biked the park. *to*
ℓ	Deletes a word or punctuation mark.	We ran around the the playground.
▭	Indicates incorrect word choice.	We had a lot of fun their *there*
◯	Indicates a misspelled word.	We plan to go agin next weekend. *again*

Answers to Masters 1–8

MASTER 1: NOUNS 1
1. newspapers, magazines, neighborhood
2. earnings, can, grandmother
3. boy, business, acquaintance, profit
4. quarterback, shortstop, forward, captain
5. school, waiter, weekends
6. man, college, business
7. luck
8. intelligence
9. persistence
10. failure
11. plan
12.–16. Answers will vary.

MASTER 2: NOUNS 2
1. William, United Airlines
2. Centralia, Illinois
3. Norwood, African American
4. Army Air Corps
5. Tuskegee Airmen
6. North Africa, Italy
7. Lori, Army Quartermaster Corps
8. Hopi, Arizona
9. Iraq War
10. Hopi, White Bear Girl
11. Piestewa Peak
12.–16. Answers will vary.

MASTER 3: VERBS 1
1. played
2. tied
3. amazed
4. batted, celebrated
5. walks, hits, steals
6. Vote, award
7. spans
8. tower
9. began
10. climbed
11. crossed
12. opened, stands
13.–22. Answers will vary. Possible answers:
13. fall
14. drop
15. close
16. run
17. dry
18. whisper
19. wake
20. leave
21. play
22. stand

MASTER 4: VERBS 2
1. past
2. future
3. present
4. future
5. past
6. present
7. past
8. sailed
9. will fish
10. harvests
11. farmed
12. will enjoy
13. pours; poured or will pour
14. dashes; dashed or will dash
15. scuttles; scuttled or will scuttle
16. snooze; snoozed or will snooze
17. surprises; surprised or will surprise
18. appear; appeared or will appear

MASTER 5: ADJECTIVES 1
1. tallest
2. busy or several
3. heavy
4. busy or several
5. brave
6. red
7. youngest
8. icy
9. frisky
10. colorful
11. Some
12. tired
13.–20. Answers will vary.

MASTER 6: ADJECTIVES 2
1. largest, great
2. first, major
3. Playful, serious
4. brilliant, every
5. yellow, quiet
6. Helpful, tall
7. old, lonely
8. sweaty, empty
9. thirsty, crisp
10. bright, ripe
11. warm, brown
12.–17. Answers will vary.

MASTER 7: ADVERBS 1
1. everywhere
2. Surprisingly
3. here
4. soundly
5. usually
6. often
7. Today
8. Surprisingly
9. soundly
10. usually
11. often
12. Today
13. everywhere
14. here
15.–19. Answers will vary. Possible answers:
15. carefully
16. eerily
17. slowly
18. bravely
19. soon

MASTER 8: ADVERBS 2
1. quickly
2. easily
3. frequently
4. gladly
5. Today
6. greatly
7. here
8. daily
9. well
10. honestly
11. always
12. deeply
13.–20. Answers will vary. Possible answers:
13. later
14. today
15. soon
16. often
17. again
18. now
19. outside
20. nearby